Rob White
S E R I E S   E D I T O R

Edward Buscombe, Colin MacCabe and David Meeker
S E R I E S   C O N S U L T A N T S

Cinema is a fragile medium. Many of the great films now exist, if at all, in damaged or incomplete prints. Concerned about the deterioration in the physical state of our film heritage, the National Film and Television Archive, part of the British Film Institute's Collections Department, has compiled a list of 360 key works in the history of the cinema. The long-term goal of the Archive is to build a collection of perfect showprints of these films, which will then be screened regularly at the National Film Theatre in London in a year-round repertory.

BFI Film Classics is a series of books intended to introduce, interpret and honour these 360 films. Critics, scholars, novelists and those distinguished in the arts have been invited to write on a film of their choice, drawn from the Archive's list. The numerous illustrations have been made specially from the Archive's own prints.

With new titles published each year, the BFI Film Classics series is a unique, authoritative and highly readable guide to the masterpieces of world cinema.

The best movie publishing idea of the [past] decade.
Philip French, *The Observer*

A remarkable series which does all kinds of varied and divergent things.
Michael Wood, *Sight and Sound*

Exquisitely dimensioned ... magnificently concentrated examples of freeform critical poetry.
Uncut

Celestial mechanics: the giant escalator 'Ethel' at Denham Studios

BFI FILM

CLASSICS

A MATTER OF LIFE AND DEATH

. . . .

Ian Christie

bfi Publishing

First published in 2000 by the
BRITISH FILM INSTITUTE
21 Stephen Street, London W1P 2LN

Copyright © Ian Christie 2000

The British Film Institute
promotes greater understanding
and appreciation of, and
access to, film and moving image
culture in the UK.

British Library Cataloguing-in-Publication Data
A catalogue record for this book is available from the British Library

ISBN 0–85170–479–4

Series design by
Andrew Barron & Collis Clements Associates

Typeset in Fournier and Franklin Gothic by
D R Bungay Associates, Burghfield, Berks

Printed in Great Britain by The Cromwell Press, Trowbridge, Wiltshire

Stills from *A Matter of Life and Death* are by courstesy of Carlton International.

The photograph on p. 27 is reproduced from J.B. Priestley, *Man & Time* (London: Aldus Books,
1964), p. 245. Eric Kennington's painting *The Heart of England* (p. 40) is reproduced from Roland
Hewison, *Literary Life in London, 1939–45* (London: Weidenfeld and Nicolson, 1977), after p. 148.
Despite considerable effort it has not been possible to trace the rights-holders in these cases.

CONTENTS

For Thelma Schoonmaker-Powell
and all Archers
here and elsewhere

To the Angels of Inconclusive Right
on both sides, to the Angel of the Last
Minutes, to the Angels of Our
Estimated Times of Arrival and Departure.
Geoffrey Hill, *The Triumph of Love* (1998)

Dunne assures us that in death we shall learn how to handle eternity successfully. We shall recover all the moments of our lives and we shall combine them as we please. God and our friends and Shakespeare will collaborate with us.
Jorge Luis Borges, 'Time and J. W. Dunne' (1952)

ACKNOWLEDGMENTS
. . . .

Many people have contributed to my understanding of *A Matter of Life and Death* over the years. Among the first were my students at Derby College of Art and Technology (now the University of Derby) in the early 70s; and most recently students on the Stanford in Oxford programme in 1995–6. At the British Film Institute, I was fortunate to have advice and help of different sorts from David Meeker, Ken Wlaschin, Clyde Jeavons, Colin McArthur and Erich Sergeant when working on various Archers projects. Like all subsequent writers on Powell and Pressburger, I have drawn heavily on Kevin Gough Yates's and Raymond Durgnat's pioneering publications; and I now admire even more John Ellis's extraordinarily prescient study of this film, 'Watching Death at Work', specially written for *Powell, Pressburger and Others*, which I edited in 1978. An invitation to talk about Powell and Pressburger at the Munich Filmmuseum in 1996 from Andreas Rost and Jan-Christopher Horak, with support from the British Council, made me think further about The Archers' wartime films; and I must thank Sian Griffiths of the *Times Higher Education Supplement* for an opportunity to write about *AMOLAD*. (Michael Powell and Emeric Pressburger always referred to the film as *AMOLAD*, just as *I Know Where I'm Going* was *IKWIG*, and in the absence of any better short titles, I have generally used these throughout the book.)

For generous access to materials from the film-makers' papers, I am grateful to Kevin McDonald and the trustees of the Pressburger estate and to Thelma Schoonmaker-Powell and the trustees of the Powell estate. I have benefited greatly from Diane Friedman's continuing research on the medical basis of the film and thank her for making this available. At a late stage in the writing, I encountered Ph.D theses by Andrew Moor and Val Wilson on The Archers, both of which I found illuminating, as was Philip Horne's Oxford seminar. I am grateful for Markku Salmi's sterling work on the credits and help with personnel research; for discussion of the film's music with Julian Philips, a recording from David Thompson, a letter from Paul Hammond and advice from Sue Nightingale, Ian Smith and Mark Fuller. The libraries of Magdalen College, Oxford, the University of Kent and Senate House, University of London were helpful and tolerant of overdue loans; the Internet Movie Database has become ever more valuable; and as usual the British Film Institute Library was indispensable as was the British Library's newspaper library.

Ed Buscombe commissioned this book longer ago than I would like to admit; and Rob White has patiently steered it to completion. I am grateful to them, as I am to my family (and to Roger and Jane), for their forbearance while the 'wrap' seemed endlessly delayed. And it *still* wouldn't have happened without Patsy.

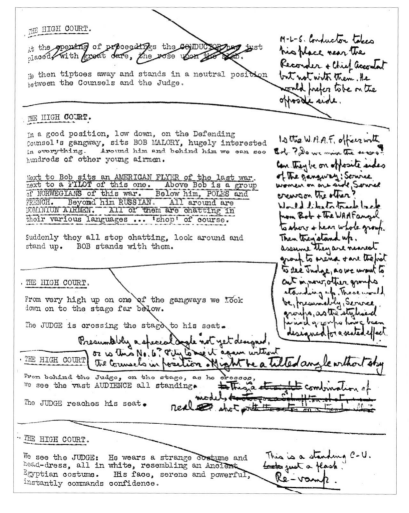

8   Annotated page from Michael Powell's shooting script

1
. . . .
BEGINNINGS

Where I Come In . . .

Having loved *A Matter of Life and Death* for over a quarter of a century, I finally had to decide how highly I rated it several years ago. A newspaper asked me to write about 'my favourite film'. I considered the options – rescuing something obscure; new light on a classic; a childhood enthusiasm revisited; Hollywood or not – before concluding that the subject of this book really had to be it.[1] What surprised me was realising how much resistance even I had to selecting a British film, putting my critical judgment where my advocate's mouth had long been. Writing the book has become an attempt to explore this unease. The result is not a close reading of the film's text, which would occupy another book, nor even a full account of its making (yet another book), but a contextual reading, aiming to place it in its own time and ours.

    A Matter of Life and Death (hereafter *AMOLAD*) has for too long been a prisoner of its founding premise. Originally conceived as wartime propaganda, it couldn't be made until after the war's end, when its message risked seeming out of date. But even if it started as a contribution to improving Anglo-American relations, there is ample evidence that its makers also had much larger and less circumstantial ambitions. And over the years, despite critical disdain and frequent regret over its propaganda aims, audiences have discovered for themselves that it is a poetic and provocative fantasy. It now ranks number twenty in the BFI's poll of the British Top 100 (and number two in the BFI Library users' poll, indicating higher status among students and scholars?). But even if it's a confirmed favourite, is it more than this? And who cares if it isn't?

    Well, *I* care, because what's at stake echoes the film's ostensible theme – defending Britain's 'cause' (or 'case') in the post-war world. Its uncertain critical reputation invites us to consider how to defend a British film against the claims of cinema's accredited classics – Eisenstein, Ford, Renoir, Welles, or Hollywood's great collaborative fantasies of the 30s and 40s.

    In at least one respect, it must be a contender. The opening of *AMOLAD* remains one of the most remarkable of any film, even by the standards of two illustrious precursors which probably influenced it – *The*

Wizard of Oz (1939) with its tornado transition from Kansas to Munchkin-land; and *Citizen Kane* (1941), which starts with an atmospheric death scene, before crashing into its brash pseudo-newsreel. *AMOLAD* begins with nothing less than a guided tour of the universe, moving us past nebulae and novae, with an authoritative, slightly amused, voice making the cosmic seem cosy: 'And here's the earth, our earth, part of the grand design. Reassuring isn't it?' But if we have been reassured, this equilibrium is abruptly shattered as we find ourselves in the wrecked cockpit of a bomber, blazing in full Technicolor, listening to its pilot's last radio exchange. Powell and Pressburger had already rehearsed this shock-beginning in their earlier '... *one of our aircraft is missing*' (1942), which starts with a mysteriously empty bomber, an aerial *Marie Celeste*, that crashes before we travel back in time to discover what happened to its missing crew.

But here there's no doubling back, no flashback reassurance. This pilot really is going to die, unless a miracle saves him – which it does in a distinctively modern way, resulting from a bureaucratic mistake of the kind only too familiar to those who had lived through the war with uncertain news of loved ones' fate. Also a ruefully patriotic one, since the pilot misses his rendezvous with death thanks to 'a real English fog'. But even before we discover his plight, we're treated to a condensed self-presentation that is more rhetorical than anything in *Kane*. The voice we hear for a full seventy seconds before we see its owner answers an imaginary questionnaire – age, education, religion, politics – as well as quoting Raleigh and Marvell to a bewildered radio operator. By the end of their passionate exchange, they have all but pledged their love in the face of the pilot's imminent death – a twist on (or merely an example of?) that other cliché of wartime romance, the kiss before dying.

Today, the effect is ultra-melodramatic, teetering on the edge of absurdity. At various public cinema screenings over the years, I have felt that familiar rising embarrassment, just held in check by the headlong bravado and humour of the writing, and by David Niven's compelling delivery. Yet the association of pilots and poetry wasn't new. A poem had provided the emotional pivot of Rattigan's and Asquith's elegiac 1944 flying drama *The Way to the Stars*.[2] And just four years later Jean Cocteau would have his modern Orpheus take dictation by car radio from beyond the grave in *Orphée*. Poetry was indeed in the air.

Then comes the film's biggest, boldest stroke, its bid for immortality. Suddenly we're in a cool modernist heaven *in black and white*, staffed by efficient WAAF-like angels and reached by escalator. Contemporary audiences may well have thought of *The Wizard of Oz*, perhaps realising this neatly reversed that film's reality / fantasy colour scheme. They might also have been reminded of the futuristic décor of Korda's *Things to Come* (1936), which had been reissued early in the war, and recalled Raymond Massey's similar roles in both films. Critics of the time recalled other 'two worlds' fantasies, such as *The Ghost Goes West* (1936), *Here Comes Mr Jordan* (1941) or *Heaven Can Wait* (1943), although few thought that *AMOLAD* measured up to these.[3] Ambitious, technically accomplished, imaginative – but ultimately shallow or silly, according to the more intellectual critics who might have been expected to appreciate it. Humphrey Swingler delivered the most scathing of the 'yes, but' verdicts:

> in *this* fantasy of two worlds the authors' continual concessions to the romantic (box-office) conception of entertainment flatten the idea behind their story. In the very first reel the effect of an exceptionally ingenious entrée to the supernatural nature of the film, via a slow panning shot across the stratosphere, is completely spoiled by an extremely tedious dialogue between doomed-bomber-pilot David Niven and an anguished WAC Kim Hunter in the conventional war-film idiom.
>
> [I]t is time that the Powell–Pressburger combination achieved something more than mere oddity; time for them perhaps to stop reaching for the moon and, if they can, plant their four feet on the earth with their contemporary technicians. For they would be in no mean company. Asquith, Carol Reed, Launder and Gilliat, the Boultings, Thorold Dickinson and David Lean among others, are establishing a tradition of solid native skill to which the latest production of this better-known combination contributes almost nothing.[4]

I quote this, not to mock its shortsightedness, but because it goes to the heart of the matter: how to mount a case for a film so out of step with other British film-making during what was felt to be a renaissance of national cinema? My defence will involve exploring the roots of the film in myth, in Shakespeare, in the tradition of masque and allegory, in English 'time culture' and 40s Neo-Romanticism, in contemporary medicine; as well as in production research being carried on within Rank, and the development of

Technicolor itself. What this will reveal is not a poor, provincial imitation of Clair, Lubitsch, Capra *et al.*, but a pioneering work both of and beyond its time. One patronised – as was Shakespeare in his own day – but now clearly able to bear an exceptional range of interpretation and analysis.[5]

Origins

Like all Powell's and Pressburger's previous joint films (although only one after, *The Red Shoes*, 1948), *AMOLAD* was an original script; and like at least four of their wartime productions, it was in some sense 'commissioned' for propaganda, or public relations purposes. Powell told the story on several occasions of how Jack Beddington, head of the film department at the Ministry of Information, had suggested over 'a very good lunch' that The Archers might tackle the theme of worsening Anglo-American relations.[6] Many in Britain had formed a negative impression of the American service personnel whose presence had grown during 1944; and during the last phase of the war, there was increasing resentment over American claims of leadership and Britain's growing economic and material dependence on its ally. The Archers were no strangers to this delicate subject, after *49th Parallel* (1941) and, more idiosyncratically, *A Canterbury Tale* (1944).[7]

According to Powell's later account, Beddington wanted 'a big film' which would, in Archers' style, 'put things the way that people understand without understanding'.[8] Pressburger duly conceived 'a real fantasy with supernatural beings', in 'a kind of surrealism' that, crucially, 'would need Technicolor'. When this proved unavailable, he quickly devised another forward-looking film that could be made in monochrome, *I Know Where I'm Going*, although this was not finished until September 1945 – by which time The Archers had already committed to *AMOLAD* (probably in January) and the end of the war was clearly in sight. Why did they revert to a propaganda piece, when conventional wisdom would have suggested that audiences needed anything but another war film?

Part of the answer is obviously that *AMOLAD*, like *IKWIG*, makes a deliberate bridge from war into peace, debating the values that will be needed in the post-war world. The opening sequence is full of topical references to the events of 1945. Although apparently set on the night of 2 May, three days before the German surrender, the commentary and dialogue refer to 'thousand bomber' attacks on German cities, which had reached a climax in February 1945; and, by implication, to the general election of July that gave Labour a mandate for sweeping reform (Peter describes his politics as 'Conservative by instinct, Labour by experience') and to the atomic bombs that were dropped on Japan in August ('someone's been messing around with the uranium atom'). Thereafter, the war recedes rapidly as the film develops its metaphysical and broad historical themes.

AMOLAD also leaves behind the realism that had framed their strictly wartime films to engage with the modernist mystique of the aviator. The 20s and 30s had seen a succession of pilots such as Charles Lindbergh and Amy Johnson become world celebrities, and artists were quick to develop a new mythology of aviation. Yeats, Brecht, Auden and Saint-Exupéry, himself a flyer, were among the writers who developed this new technological chivalry.[9] Among 30s film-makers, Pudovkin celebrated aviators as the new explorers in *Victory* (1938); while Hawks and Renoir both portrayed the new self-deprecating style of heroism associated with flyers in *Only Angels Have Wings* and *La Régle du jeu* (both 1939).[10]

The fighter pilots of the Battle of Britain became the first popular heroes of the war, followed by the bomber crews whom Powell and Pressburger celebrated in '... *one of our aircraft is missing*' and the flyers of the Fleet Air Arm, for which they made a recruiting film, *The Volunteer*, in 1943. How vividly this new heroism was felt emerges from a short film Powell made impulsively in 1941, responding to a letter published posthumously in *The Times*. The text of *An Airman's Letter to his Mother* reinstates the elevated patriotism of '*dulce et decorum est pro patria mori*' as if the First World War poets had never questioned it, amplified by John Gielgud's intense delivery.[11] The airman of 1940 expected his mother to take comfort from knowing that he had played an important part in the war effort and 'to accept the facts [of his death] dispassionately', admonishing her not to grieve for him, 'for if you really believe in religion and all that it entails that would be hypocrisy'. *AMOLAD*'s Peter Carter is less priggish, asking June to convey what he could not say to his mother in life:

> Tell her that I love her. You'll have to write this for me. ... I want her to know that I love her very much – even though I've never shown it, but I've loved her always – right to the end.

The *Times* letter offers a remarkable insight into a certain vein of English wartime ideology: a mixture of imperial and patriotic pride, Christian stoicism combined with a mystical sense of destiny that leads easily to the eschatological framing of *AMOLAD*:

> History resounds with illustrious names who have given all, yet their sacrifice has resulted in the British Empire, where there is a measure of peace, justice and freedom for all. ...
>
> I still maintain that this war is a very good thing; every individual is having the chance to give and dare all for his principle like the martyrs of old. ... I have no fear of death; only a queer elation. ... The universe is so vast and so ageless that the life of one man can only be justified by the measure of his sacrifice. We are sent to this world to acquire a personality and a character to take with us that can never be taken from us ... with the final test of war, I consider my character fully developed. Thus at my early age my earthly mission is already fulfilled. ...

By comparison, *AMOLAD* is modest, humorous, less sure of Britain's place in the post-war world; but its cosmology is similar, and the 1940 airman's reference to his 'earthly mission' seems almost to invite an exploration of its eternal counterpart.

Another real-life, and more cynical, instance of this mystical fatalism was the pilot Richard Hillary, who survived a crash and severe disfigurement, to write a bestseller, *The Last Enemy*, before dying in another crash at the age of twenty-three in 1943. Hillary wrote of belonging to a 'lost generation' which had welcomed the war as a surrogate 'Holy Grail ... in a delightfully palatable form': 'it demanded no heroics, but gave us the opportunity to demonstrate in action our dislike of organized emotion and patriotism, the opportunity to prove ourselves'.[12] Arthur Koestler, a Hungarian friend of Pressburger, identified the influence on Hillary of T. E. Lawrence's romantic myth and also of his own theory of two planes of existence, the '*vie triviale*' and, 'in moments of danger, elation etc. ... the *vie tragique*, with its un-commonsense cosmic perspective' – a phrase that could well define *AMOLAD*.[13] The potent mythology of the knight-pilot was a theme that would continue to preoccupy both Archers.[14]

A Modern Masque
A British rear gunner was reported by German radio in 1944 as having landed unhurt in a snowdrift after falling 18,000 feet from a Lancaster.[15]

From this 'believe it or not' anecdote, Pressburger conceived a supernat-ural fantasy, which he then developed when *IKWIG* was in production and Powell reworked during his voyage to New York in early May.[16] 'Emeric had done the historical research and written the story and most of the jokes,' while Powell had researched the medical background and 'brought to the script all that I knew and loved about England', including a range of poetry quotations. Powell recalled Pressburger 'a little dismayed when he saw how thin the script had become, but when he read it he was enthusias-tic'.[17] Judging from the difference between all known versions of the script and the final film, this process of revision must have continued throughout production.

The main problem facing The Archers at this point was how to dramatise the schematic structure of a romantic couple whose love is (a) threatened by the man's likely death from war injury, then reprieved by a successful operation; and (b) forbidden by the law of mortality, then allowed after an appeal before heaven's court. As an allegory of the situa-tion at the end of the war it works well: a dying English hero is saved by the love of a 'vibrant' American girl, (a) supported by the sacrifice of an English doctor and American surgeon, and (b) vindicated by an American jury, after hearing the case for and against put by an 'average' Englishman and an American bigot. The film's structural novelty consists in its coun-terpoint of the factual/medical and the fantasy/hallucination, both of which we are encouraged to consider equally 'real'. This sets it somewhat apart from the spate of 30s 'living ghost' films, typified by *Topper* (1937), and the symptomatic dreams, as in *Lady in the Dark* (1944) and *Spellbound* (1946), that were equally characteristic of the 40s.

But there is an inevitable tension in allegory between the demands of narrative sufficiency and allusive implication. *AMOLAD* in fact uses a range of figural strategies to signal its intentions. The second poet quoted by Peter is Andrew Marvell, one of the 'Metaphysicals' who prompted Johnson's definition of the poetic 'conceit' as proposing 'occult resem-blances between things apparently unlike'.[18] And the parallelism between operating theatre and heavenly court, doctor and counsel, surgeon and judge recalls the classical epic simile that Pope parodied in the parallel mil-itary and amorous 'campaigns' of his *Rape of the Lock*.[19] Similarly, the giant escalator which gives the film its most striking image evokes Jacob's Ladder from Genesis, or its reappearance in English literature's most famous allegory, *The Pilgrim's Progress*.

David Mellor has argued that the outbreak of war produced a 'new symbolic order' in British war-related art, with even non-fiction film-makers moving towards 'a documentarist-baroque in which the rhetorical modes of Pageants, Triumphs and Masques could be remobilised under the ideological aegis of the Churchillian renaissance'.[20] Even more explicitly than a documentarist such as Jennings, I think The Archers can be seen as part of this movement, with both *Blimp* and *AMOLAD* striking examples of the reinvention of the masque. This form of spectacle, combining elements of verse drama, dance, music, scenery and costume, was popular in aristocratic and court circles in the sixteenth and seventeenth centuries. Masques were usually allegorical, with a mythological scenario which could also be read in terms of contemporary politics. The court masque reached its height during the reign of James I, with the playwright Ben Jonson developing its dramatic structure by adding a comic prelude or 'anti-masque', and the architect Inigo Jones using the almost unlimited funds available to introduce for the first time all the machinery of modern theatre – artificial lighting, moveable sets and magical effects – to create 'pictures with Light and Motion'.[21] The fact that these only existed *as* performance explains why English literary history has preferred to celebrate the text-based popular Elizabethan and Jacobean public theatre, but even this is not devoid of masque-like elements – and one such example supports my claim that *AMOLAD* is, in some sense, *meant* as a masque.

As first written, the powerful scene in which Dr Reeves examines Peter and takes on his case was set in a 'loggia' at Lee Wood House, and involved only Peter, Reeves and June. The shooting script added as background 'a bunch of American girls and boys ... rehearsing a play or concert', which became in the film a fully-fledged 'quotation' from Shakespeare's *A Midsummer Night's Dream*, improvised at short notice, according to one of the actors.[22] Mendelssohn's familiar incidental music sets the scene, before some banter over misspelling Shakespeare leads to a comic rehearsal of the Mechanicals' own rehearsal scene for their 'lamentable comedy' (III.1), led by an ebullient English vicar.[23] Two close-ups punctuate the scene – of the Mendelssohn disc finishing, followed by a pianist's hand playing the ominous 'Hereafter' theme – as the rehearsal becomes a silent but still visible background to Peter and June playing chess in another part of the great hall while they await Dr Reeves.

This new prelude to the scene is rich in associations. Most obviously, it evokes a history of Anglo-American cultural unease over

Shakespeare, satirised as early as 1916 in a film by J. M. Barrie.[24] Here we have the vicar's plummy English voice, of the kind traditionally associated with Shakespeare, chiding an American serviceman for playing Bottom 'like a gangster' – unmistakably recalling Jimmy Cagney as Bottom in Reinhardt and Dieterle's 1935 Hollywood *A Midsummer Night's Dream*. A reminder of the culture shared by these two English-speaking nations? At any rate, a scene which amplifies the general theme of how *mis*understanding can arise between England and America.

But equally important is the *formal* presence of this prelude to the main scene, in which we learn about Peter as a pilot and poet, and also about the medical hypothesis that will 'explain' his hallucinations and give them rational status. The vast hall recalls the aristocratic setting for much Elizabethan and Jacobean courtly entertainment. And *A Midsummer Night's Dream* itself, although generally believed to have been intended for the public playhouse, has undeniable elements of the kind of masque that would be devised in the seventeenth century to celebrate weddings.[25]

The *Dream*'s general theme of 'true' marital choices temporarily frustrated by magic and mischief clearly rhymes with *AMOLAD*'s own romantic plot; while the fairy-tale coincidences of Peter discovering June, first ethereally by radio and then physically on the beach, also echo the *Dream*'s world of romantic masquerade. But the closest similarity is the heavenly messenger Conductor 71, whose magical powers suggest a combination of the *Dream*'s Puck and Prospero's servant Ariel in *The Tempest*. Like Shakespeare's fantasy plays, *AMOLAD* needs magic conventions: so Conductor 71 can only be seen by those within heaven's domain, and he has the power to stop, or even reverse, time. One of the film's only two exotic characters (the other is the American revolutionary, Abraham Farlan), he is a guillotined 'aristo' from the French Revolution in full period costume played by Marius Goring with an exaggerated accent. Like Shakespeare's captive spirits, he is only the servant of a higher power, and fallible – it was his failure to 'collect' Peter in the fog over the English Channel that led to the meeting with June and Peter's petition to stay on earth.

A second major visual elaboration of the original script occurs in the scene immediately following Conductor 71's first visit, when June visits Dr Reeves and introduces this third main character. In the draft, this is simply a conversation in the doctor's study; but in the film it is memorably transposed to a camera obscura, from which Dr Reeves can survey what June calls, jokingly, his 'kingdom'.[26] The immediate association of this *coup de cinéma* is back to the opening scene in heaven, where Sgt Trubshaw has been able to look down at the ant-like ranks of clerks working on the records of the living; but it also evokes Prospero, maintaining surveillance over his island kingdom in *The Tempest* – and in Powell's later unfilmed adaptation of the play, Prospero explicitly uses mirrors to control the island.[27] Reeves keeps a benevolent, diagnostic eye on his patients through the camera obscura that is his hobby. In this respect, he is a more benign version of Thomas Colpeper, the magistrate in *A Canterbury Tale*, who campaigns to spread awareness of local history, using a magic lantern in his lectures.

In the film's pivotal dramatic turn, Reeves is killed while trying to get Peter to hospital, which 'qualifies' him to become Peter's advocate in heaven, while the notes he has left guide the operation that saves Peter's life on earth. There is for most viewers, I think, a strong sense of inevitability about this pattern, which quite removes any sense of tragedy from Reeves's death. It is intended to, and does, seem like the fulfilment of destiny; and so this magician-scientist figure enters the realm of myth. *AMOLAD* may have no single mythic source, but there are at least echoes of Orpheus and Eurydice – albeit with roles reversed, as this Eurydice seeks to save her poet from the nether world – and perhaps more of Euripides's *Alcestis*, again with the gender roles reversed. In Euripides, Admetis's wife Alcestis has volunteered to die in his place, leaving him heartbroken.[28] When Hercules discovers this, he brings Alcestis back from Hades, but in disguise, to test Admetis's sincerity, before reuniting them. In *AMOLAD*, at the climax of the trial/operation, June is asked by Dr Reeves if she will take Peter's place, which she accepts, thus clinching the defence case that the couple's love is true.

It is by means of this mythic association, together with the invocation of motifs from the two Shakespearean 'magic' plays, *A Midsummer Night's Dream* and *The Tempest*, that *AMOLAD* creates its masque-like story. Its characters are indeed not realistic individuals, even by the standards of 40s cinema, but are emblematic and allegorical: the Poet, his Beloved, the Heavenly Messenger, the Magician. They move in equally symbolic spaces: the Other World; and on earth, the Seashore, the Wood, the Palace, and that modern temple of mysteries, the hospital. And the machinery of the spectacle – most notably the giant escalator and the celestial amphitheatre, but also such an ultra-filmic effect as the giant eyelid closing over the screen under anaesthesia – is as important as were Jones's stage 'machines' for Jacobean masques.

In truth, such stylisation had become almost commonplace in other forms of drama during the decade before *AMOLAD*, even if it was still rare on screen. Brecht's didactic *lehrstücke* and other experiments in combining music and drama influenced Auden's and Isherwood's experimental work for the Group Theatre in the mid-30s;[29] while T. S. Eliot had two unexpected theatrical successes with *The Rock* (1934), a time-travelling pageant, and *Murder in the Cathedral* (1935), which transferred from Canterbury Cathedral to the West End and was broadcast by the BBC to acclaim in 1936.[30] J. B. Priestley's 'time plays' will be discussed later, but even he was not immune to the vogue for stylisation. His *Johnson Over Jordan* (1939) was a bold attempt at a modern morality, in which the central character reviews his life after death, designed by Gordon Craig using stark cycloramas and with music by Benjamin Britten. Vaughan Williams, leader of the nationalist school of English composers, had subtitled his 1930 ballet *Job* 'a masque for dancing'. Meanwhile, the pageant form was revived by E. M. Forster in *England's Pleasant Land* (1938) and served as a complex metaphor for English history and culture in Virginia Woolf's last novel, *Between the Acts*, written in 1941 and shaped by Woolf's ambivalent attitude towards popular patriotism and village-hall drama.[31]

Radio had become a new stimulus to experimentation, freeing drama from stagebound linearity and redundancy: Louis MacNeice's and Dallas Bower's *Alexander Nevsky* (1941), adapted from Eisenstein's film, inaugurated a series of verse epics with integral music. *AMOLAD* acknowledges how important radio had become during the war, from its opening sound montage of such familiar voices as Churchill's and Hitler's to the radio 'evidence' offered during Peter's trial. In the week after the film's premiere, the new BBC Third Programme broadcast an experimental dramatised feature on atomic energy and an 'imaginary conversation' between Napoleon and his aides.

Powell and Pressburger had already embarked on their own form of modernised allegory in *Blimp*, bringing the popular cartoon character to life as an emblem of England challenged by 'total war'. One of that film's devices is its hero's attendance at a performance of *Ulysses*, echoing the theme of the soldier's long-delayed homecoming.[32] This device, known as *mis en abyme*, is effectively the function served by the *Midsummer Night's Dream* extract (a rehearsal of a rehearsal-within-a-play) and the

camera obscura's 'doubling' of filmic observation in *AMOLAD*, both moti-
vating our non-naturalistic reading of the film.[33]

Sources and Parallels
One of many mysteries surrounding the genesis of *AMOLAD* is exactly
what part was played by the Hungarian writer Frigyes Karinthy's remarkable account of his brain tumour, first published in 1937 and translated
into English in the following year as *Journey Round My Skull*.[34] Whatever
the sequence of events, Karinthy's account of his vivid hallucinations,
from the first sound of trains, 'loud, insistent, continuous ... powerful
enough to drown out real sounds', to the fully audio-visual, is certainly
suggestive.[35]

The climax of the book is an operation, during which Karinthy
remained mostly conscious, although his account of it moves freely into
fantasy which, significantly, 'come[s] before my eyes like a sequence from
a film ... a film of memory images embedded amongst the ganglions and
convolutions of my brain. ... The hallucination consisted in my mind
seeming to move freely about the room'.[36] After he imagines seeing the
tumour removed, there is an episode in which the surgeon seems 'to
manipulate the pegs and controls of a telephone exchange on the switchboard of my open brain'. An ever-increasing babble of messages
threatens to jam the switchboard: 'what arguments, what battles, what
demands, entreaties and threats came flashing over the wires!' Then 'a foreign country put through a request for a line', and this insistent foreign
voice demands priority: 'Answer me at once! I want a definite "yes" or
"no".' The demand reaches a crescendo, until a fuse blows and 'deathly
silence' follows.[37] The surgeon seems to whisper that the tumour was the
result of his argumentative temperament, which recalls the memory of
childhood injustices: 'When I was only a child ... they used to punish
me. ... Nobody listened to my defence. ...'

Here, conceivably, is the kernel of *AMOLAD*'s mapping of a brain
operation onto a process of self-justification in the form of a 'trial'. At any
rate, there can be little doubt of the influence of Karinthy's vivid account
of a series of hallucinations, including one in which he is 'visited' by a
mysterious doctor who arranges a test that would have been fatal if carried out. This chapter, which he likens to a dream, is called 'Death Tempts
Me'; and it has the same sense of a trap being sprung as the Conductor's
attempts to lure Peter to heaven in the escalator scene. Feeling lost in space

and time, as Karinthy eloquently describes it, is another important contribution to the hallucinatory structure of *AMOLAD*.

Karinthy, however, was not the only source of the film's medical
structure. Powell turned to medical textbooks when he could see no way
of filming the draft script's unsupported fantasy.

> Out of these I got the facts that hallucinations take place not in time
> but in space. That was a turning point because that meant I could stop
> time. And then there were all the other things like the pressure on the
> eyes and the smell of fried onions, which all came from textbooks.[38]

The source of this advice was Powell's brother-in-law, Joseph Reidy, a
leading plastic surgeon during the war, who apparently lent him a pamphlet containing the germ of the hallucination idea.[39] But how much
would a plastic surgeon know about neurology? Diane Broadbent
Friedman has identified both the likely source of expertise and some of the
texts that Powell may have read. Reidy worked closely with Dr Hugh
Cairns, then Professor of Neurology at Oxford – 'he would deal with the
brain injuries and I would deal with the external cover' – and Powell may
even have made hospital rounds with Cairns.[40] Friedman's initial diagnosis was that Peter has suffered a complex partial seizure, which would
encompass detailed audiovisual hallucinations, an olfactory hallucination
(the smell of fried onions that heralds the Conductor's 'appearances'),
and a shrinkage of the visual field (which Dr Reeves tests in the meeting at
Lee Wood House).

Having delved further into the literature that Reidy or Cairns may
have offered Powell, Friedman concludes that the Reeves's 'diagnosis' is
even more coherent and referenced than she suspected. One article in particular, from 1939, mentioned Karinthy's book and referred to 'a case
which begins with an hallucination of smell', as well as reporting Hugh
Cairns's survey of 800 cases of intracranial tumour, of which 'about 100
had experienced visual hallucination'. Cairns observed that '[m]ore complex hallucinations related always to past experience; it is the diplomat
who served in Japan and not the cook from Whitechapel who sees the
Japanese warrior in tortoiseshell armour.'[41] Hence the historian Peter
Carter's historically informed hallucination, with figures from the French
and American revolutions; and also Dr Reeves's insistence to the hospital
doctor that Peter's hallucinations 'never go beyond the limits of his

imagination' and are 'invention, but logical'. There are also frequent mentions of cinema, in Karinthy – who recorded seeing a film of a brain operation by the pioneer surgeon Cushing before his diagnosis – and in the medical writings on hallucination of the 30s and 40s.

Pressburger's pencil draft already contained the basic premise, the characters and much of the dramatic structure and progression. Some of its minor differences point towards other likely influences. Heaven is more detailed in the draft, with an elaborate accountants' department seen at work; and this recalls that one of Pressburger's early scripts was another heavenly fantasy, *I'd Rather Have Cod Liver Oil*, co-written with Erich Kästner and the first film to be directed by Max Ophuls.[42] The theme is also a celestial mistake: St Peter decides to grant a prayer while God is away, and when a child asks why he has to do everything his parents want, Peter 'goes into a machine room full of complicated instruments and exchanges the cards marked "parental authority" and "filial obedience"'. In Pressburger's draft, the Conductor is a 'collector', recalling the sinister figure in E. T. A. Hoffmann's story 'The Sand-Man' who collects children and souls, later to be brought to the screen in The Archers' *Tales of Hoffmann* (1951).[43]

Powell's experience of working on *The Thief of Bagdad* (1940) had given him a strong taste for spectacle and fantasy; but between *AMOLAD*'s conception and realisation, *A Canterbury Tale* had met with hostile incomprehension, no doubt partly because its allegorical dimension was subordinated to a nominal realism. Powell drew the conclusion that fantasy needed to be clearly signalled and 'justified' by a framework of recognisable conventions. And as a lifelong Kipling enthusiast, he would have known the First World War story 'On the Gate', which portrays heaven's administration hard pressed by the flood of casualties resulting from the war.[44] The story's basic technique is to mask its religious and moral concerns in a gruff version of military-colonial parlance, with a minimum of narrative incident (a 'volunteer' in the Death Offices is unmasked as a subversive 'Imp of the Pit'; an Importunate Widow pushes her dead son forward as a candidate for the heavenly choir, etc.), set in a fantastic empyrean which combines Renaissance marble and Victoria Station against a celestial backdrop, pointing towards the modernised heaven of *AMOLAD*. As in the film, irreverent jokes undercut solemnity and sentimentality, while anachronisms, such as a 'recorder [sparking] furiously a broken run of S.O.S.s', mingle with images drawn from traditional Christian and mythological iconography ('a Love in Armour, stamping his mailed foot'). Here, in effect, is an early version of *AMOLAD*'s bureaucratic, yet still awesome, vision.

Kipling's heaven is clearly Christian, despite its vernacular novelty, but many early twentieth-century supernatural fantasies were distinctly secular. Among these, E. M. Forster's stories 'The Celestial Omnibus' and 'Co-Ordination' both confront conventional piety about the afterlife with comic bathos – in the former, a boy from Surbiton successfully makes a round-trip bus journey to Heaven (driven by Sir Thomas Browne), while a pretentious neighbour dies from disbelief in his alleged heroes; and in the latter, Beethoven and Napoleon watch approvingly as their achievements are endlessly rehearsed below in a progressive educational experiment at a girl's school, intended to impress the Board of Education. These belong to the common culture from which *AMOLAD* sprang, revealing how much it traded on an ambivalent play with the supernatural. Coincidentally, when Forster collected his stories in 1947, he dedicated the book to Hermes, 'who used to do the smaller behests of the gods – messenger, machine-breaker, and conductor of souls to a not-too-terrible hereafter'.[45]

Metaphysics
However much *AMOLAD* was re-written and researched to 'ground' its fantasy, few viewers have doubted that it still carries a poetic, if not mystical, message. A clue to this intended dimension of the film appears as an epigraph to the shooting script:

> There is a music wherever there is a harmony, order or proportion; and thus far we may maintain the Music of the Spheres; for those well-ordered motions, and regular paces, though they give no sound unto the ear, yet to the understanding they strike a note most full of harmony.

This is from *Religio Medici*, a meditation by the seventeenth-century physician and essayist Sir Thomas Browne, whose writings combined Christian piety, vaulting imagination and classical erudition.[46] His influential essay views man as a microcosm of the universe and stresses the importance of toleration and respect for other nations – all highly relevant to *AMOLAD* – but even more significant is its uniquely visionary quality. 'I love to lose my selfe in a mystery to pursue my reason to an *oh altitudo*', confessed Browne, and much of his writings' resonance is due to a sturdy Anglicanism clothed in a rhetoric which frankly admits the lure of Neo-Platonic and hermetic mysticism.[47]

The quotation from Browne sanctions an interpretation of Reeves as a source of both medical and metaphysical wisdom, a mediator between two worlds. A neurologist, apparently of some distinction, a seer and a connoisseur of literature: like a Renaissance magus, he bestrides the outer and inner worlds. When he arrives in heaven after a fatal crash, his first guide is the author of *The Pilgrim's Progress*. Like a visual epigraph, Bunyan serves to trigger a series of associations, recalling that Peter identifies himself as a pilgrim in the opening scene by quoting Raleigh: 'Give me my scallop shell of quiet … / And thus I'll take my pilgrimage.'[48]

The Pilgrim's Progress can be seen as a kind of sacred novel for those sections of nonconformist society which would have been deeply suspicious of secular fiction (or of the classicised world of Dante's *Divine Comedy*, another allegorical pilgrimage with a poet as protagonist); and Bunyan's allegorical characters and settings – Mr Stand-fast, Valiant-for Truth, Vanity Fair, the Slough of Despond – quickly became cornerstones of English vernacular culture, as the book became a semi-official companion to the Bible itself. But why the specific reference in *AMOLAD*?

The simplest answer would be that Powell and Pressburger were reported to be planning a film of *The Pilgrim's Progress* in 1943.[49] Whether this was ever a serious project, or an intended favour to their main sponsor, Arthur Rank, is not clear. Certainly Rank had long wanted to produce *The Pilgrim's Progress*, and a version was eventually made by a Rank subsidiary as two short films of ten and seventeen minutes in 1950–1, using static drawings and voice-over with music by Handel.[50] However, The Archers had already tackled the theme of modern 'pilgrimage' in *A Canterbury Tale*, in which their latter-day pilgrims, far removed from Chaucer's motley band, were united by a common search for values and new bearings, made possible by the upheaval of the war. They spoke of it in later life as part of a 'crusade against materialism'; and this is clearly the spirit that motivates the hero and eventually the heroine of *IKWIG*. Peter Carter seems to be cast in the same mould, when he announces his belief that the next world 'starts where this one leaves off. Or where this one could leave off if we'd listened to Plato and Aristotle and Jesus, with all our little earthly problems solved, but with greater ones worth the solving.'

Peter's 'next world' is a projection of his ideals: a place where injustice and prejudice can be challenged and set right; where love can overrule law. Like Bunyan's pilgrim, Christian, he has suffered yet persevered in his search for 'salvation'. He has been tempted to give in – though it is a heavenly messenger who has tempted him – but thanks to his advocate Dr Reeves, endorsed by Bunyan himself – he wins through.

The Pilgrim's Progress may also illuminate the film's most striking visual motif: the giant escalator that links earth and heaven. In the second part of Bunyan's allegory, the pilgrim's wife Christiana sees the same vision that Jacob has in Genesis 26.6, when he dreams of 'a ladder set up on the earth, and the top of it reached to heaven; and behold the angels of God ascending and descending on it'. One of four inspirational images shown to Christiana and her family as they journey to the Celestial City, it is a scene traditionally visualised in the work's illustrated editions.[51] In the same nonconformist visionary tradition as Bunyan, William Blake pictured in one of the plates of his series *The Gates of Paradise* a ladder rising from the earth to the crescent moon, with a figure setting out on it, watched by others, and the caption 'I want! I want'.[52] Much later, a similar tradition would produce what is probably the founding 'ladder' image in cinema. This occurs in the Victor Sjöstrom's *The Sons of Ingmar* (1919), when 'Little Ingmar' pauses in his ploughing and decides to consult his dead father in heaven, at which point a ladder appears and he climbs up to a homely Valhalla peopled by preceding generations of Ingmars.[53] But there is nothing sinister in this rustic symbol of continuity between past and present: Ingmar returns from his dream empowered to face his responsibilities and become the next 'big Ingmar' in his line.

Pressburger's first draft stops before Reeves's death, with the line 'My dear friend, here on Earth, I'm your defending counsel', and no indication as to how the subsequent parallel between operation on earth and appeal in heaven would be elaborated. In terms of poetic imagery, the rose bearing June's tear – described by Reeves as 'our only real evidence' – seems highly significant. Could this be another reference, conscious or otherwise, to Blake? Less to the 'Sick Rose' of the *Songs of Experience* than to Blake's microcosm–macrocosm mysticism: 'To see ... Heaven in a Wild Flower/Hold Infinity in the palm of your hand.'[54]

Like the silver rose in Hoffmanstahl's and Strauss's *Der Rosenkavalier*, the evidential rose of *AMOLAD* is a complex symbol, combining the erotic, the sacramental and the metaphysical. Plucked from the

Conductor's buttonhole, it bears June's tear from the 'real' coloured world to the etiolated grey of the other world: a visible token of her love to set against prejudice, rhetoric, law; and also an emblem of transformation, as colour drains from it before our eyes, evoking the mysterious traditions of alchemy and Rosicrucianism that stand behind the film's pageantry.[55]

Speculation about access to a deeper knowledge than the merely pragmatic was as common among secular progressives as religious mystics at the turn of the century. H. G. Wells's story 'The Dream of Armageddon' tells of a man haunted by vivid serial dreams of a future catastrophe in which he dies. And in the early 30s, he returned to this prophetic mode with a 'history of the future' in the form of a fictitious dream diary, *The Shape of Things to Come*, tracing the imagined destruction of European civilisation through war and its rebirth as an enlightened dictatorship by airmen-philosophers. Korda's lavish production based on the book, *Things to Come*, offered a filmic vision of the future metropolis that is clearly echoed in the design of *AMOLAD*'s heaven, as well as reinforcing the mystique of the aviator. Wells's fellow Fabian, George Bernard Shaw, deployed a similar blend of didacticism and fantasy, albeit with more humour; and his *Man and Superman* (1903) contains a virtual blueprint for *AMOLAD*'s trial. In the third act, the play's modern characters are recast as sixteenth-century equivalents in a Parliament in Hell, set 'Beyond Space, Beyond Time', where Don Juan debates human perfectibility with the Devil – very much like Frank Reeves against Abraham Farlan.

Immortality was also the concern of the seekers and scholars who formed the Society for Psychical Research in 1882, to investigate scientifically paranormal evidence of communication between the living and the dead. The culmination of this movement was Frederic Myers's treatise *Human Personality and Its Survival of Bodily Death*, whose title is echoed in the question that Dr Reeves puts to Peter at their first meeting: 'Do you believe in the survival of the human personality after death?', which is answered affirmatively with 'I thought you'd read my poetry'. When June admits that she hasn't thought about it, Reeves says that he has 'thought about it too much'.[56] The implication appears to be a shared hope between the poet and doctor, who recognise each other as fellow-believers, committed to, in Myers's phrase, 'deciphering that open secret'. Myers struggled, like many Victorians, to reconcile science and religion; and his conclusion, that 'religion, in its most permanent sense, is the adjustment of our emotions to the structure of the universe', would clearly suit Reeves, who tells Dr McEwan that he's been taking notes on the Next World from Peter's account of it.[57] And this is vitally important for the narrative's most daring turn: for unless we also accept that Dr Reeves has in some sense 'survived' his death – and, despite the film's opening disclaimer, that its afterlife has some reality other than in Peter's hallucination – then Reeves's death will be tragic and pointless, instead of purposeful, as it appears in the film.

The idea of 'going ahead' is of course established in the New Testament and in the journey narrative of *The Pilgrim's Progress*.[58] But the 20s and 30s saw a number of new theories of time as in some way manipulable, which proved highly popular and provide the immediate background to *AMOLAD*'s 'cool' or agnostic mysticism, as expressed by the Conductor's, 'What is time? A mere trifle.' The most pervasive of these was *An Experiment with Time* (1927) by a former aircraft designer, J. W. Dunne, in which he outlined a theory of the possibility of precognition through dream-recording based upon a spatial conception of time.[59] Dunne influenced a series of plays by J. B. Priestley – *Dangerous Corner* (1932), *Time and the Conways* and *I Have Been Here Before* (both 1937), *An Inspector Calls* and *The Linden Tree* (both 1947) – in which time is treated as multiple or conditional. Characters are shown the consequences of their actions, and these may be undone or revised. In a distinct

Time theorist J. W. Dunne with J. B. Priestley during the rehearsal of *Time and the Conways* in 1937

echo of this schema, Peter not only 'wins' the right to live, but is allotted a fixed time with June.

While ideas such as Dunne's and Priestley's appealed to the commonsensical, intrigued only by temporal paradoxes, the war seems to have stimulated a renewed appetite for mysticism, as indeed the First World War had stimulated interest in spiritualism.[60] 'Out of time' experience is central to such works as the Boultings' *Thunder Rock* (1942), in which a lighthouse keeper is besieged by accusing ghosts; and *The Halfway House* (1944), whose occupants are given a chance to rethink their lives;[61] while the most frequently cited 'two worlds' films that immediately predated *AMOLAD*, *Heaven Can Wait* and *Here Comes Mr Jordan*, were both wartime productions, although not war-related – unlike *A Guy Named Joe* (1944), which will be discussed later.

AMOLAD was indeed an 'original' script, but one also shaped by many influences and traditions, cultural, religious and scientific. It can no more be contained by reference to its 'commission' by the Ministry of Information than can, say, Spenser's *Faerie Queen* or Shakespeare's history plays in terms of Tudor propaganda. Nor need it be seen only in terms of 'a conjuring trick' or 'a tilt at the documentary boys', as Powell spoke of it in various late interviews, although it is these too. But in the first place, it was a complex production to be mounted amid the exhaustion of the months following 'victory', as Britain faced up to the war's toll on its morale and economy.

2

. . . .

PRODUCTION

Independence

AMOLAD began shooting on 14 August 1945, the day that Japan surrendered. Its wartime justification had gone, but the underlying issue of Anglo-American relations was, if anything, even more fraught. Effectively bankrupt, Britain had to negotiate terms with the US to pay back what had been loaned and leased, while trying to rebuild its economy. Cinema attendance was at its height – 30 million admissions per week – and £17 million of box-office revenue was being remitted annually to the US.[62] In the year following *AMOLAD*'s release, a government move to tax film earnings would lead to a boycott by Hollywood, followed by a climbdown which further depressed the struggling British industry.

Before and during this crisis, much of that industry was controlled by J. Arthur Rank; and it was he who approved *AMOLAD*, as he had Powell and Pressburger's three previous films, also made under the banner of The Archers and released through Rank's General Film Distributors to the Rank Odeon circuit of cinemas. But Rank was no ordinary tycoon. As well as being heir to a flour-milling empire, he was also a devout Methodist and it was through supplying film projectors to churches that he first became aware of British cinema's endemic problems. Having co-produced a Yorkshire fishing village drama, *The Turn of the Tide*, in 1935, he discovered that the cartel structure of the British distribution trade made covering the costs of even a Venice festival prize-winner almost impossible. Looking at the cinema as a business, in the spirit of Weber's 'protestant ethic', he saw no contradiction in feeling 'guided by God'.[63] In doing so, he also brought a modern corporate outlook for the first time to Britain's stunted film industry.

After taking over General Film Distributors in 1935, a series of shrewd moves gave him effective control of three major studios and two of the three national cinema chains by 1941. By this stage, he could no longer run his vast film interests part-time, so he became full-time chairman of the network of interrelated companies, with John Davis as chief executive. One vital element, however, was missing – a regular supply of suitable productions to occupy the studios, and feed the distribution and exhibition system.

Here, again, business and ideology ran in tandem. Although American films continued to account for the bulk of cinema admissions, as they had done since the 1910s, there was greater public interest in British-made films that spoke of and to the war situation. And Rank firmly believed that there was a need for more wholesome films on British themes (as well as the tax advantage of being able to off-set production costs against large profits from exhibition). Meanwhile, Powell and Pressburger realised that their increasingly ambitious plans needed more consistent backing. They were still finishing '… one of our aircraft is missing', when they had two crucial meetings with Rank in January 1942, organised by their agent, Christopher Mann. Pressburger recorded in his diary: 'It was a triumph! We agreed on making 2 pictures for them in the next year, subject to our discretion (first *Blimp*) with £15,000 per picture, plus 10% from the net profit. There was not much discussion about it.'[64]

Powell and Pressburger now became The Archers, and were joined as founder members of Independent Producers Ltd by the producer Marcel Hellman, actor turned producer Leslie Howard, and A. W. Watkins, a sound recordist. The aim, according to a press report in August, was to 'promote business co-operation between the various producers concerned, and to provide the machinery to enable them to make the best use of the manpower and studio space'.[65] Powell and Pressburger next invited two newly-formed groups, Cineguild and Individual Pictures, both consisting of film-makers wanting greater control over their work who were also old friends. Of Cineguild's Anthony Havelock-Alan, David Lean and Ronald Neame, the latter two had worked with Powell and Pressburger (most recently as editor and cinematographer of '… one of our aircraft is missing'), before making their mark with Noël Coward's *In Which We Serve* (1942); while Individual's Frank Launder and Sidney Gilliat were both established screenwriters who had already ventured into Archers-style collaboration with the Home Front panorama *Millions Like Us* (1943). Other members were George Bernard Shaw's protégé Gabriel Pascal and the documentarist Ian Dalrymple.

Independent Producers' output would include many of British cinema's 40s classics, including *The Life and Death of Colonel Blimp*, *Henry V*, *Caesar and Cleopatra*, *Brief Encounter*, *The Rake's Progress*, *Great Expectations* and *Black Narcissus*. For film-makers who had survived the privations of the 30s, it was almost too good to be true — and there is an unmistakable pride in an article by Powell and Pressburger for *Variety* in January 1944:

> All kinds of craftsmen are taking responsibility for making the current list of films: writers, actors, directors, cameramen, editors – and we mean sole responsibility for conceiving, planning and delivering the film to the distributor each ... in his own way.

This extraordinary freedom combined with financial security undoubtedly accelerated Powell and Pressburger's rapid creative development from 1942. And, in turn, the rapport between Arthur Rank and The Archers, sharing a concern with English values and a hostility to 'materialism', seems to have been an important inspiration for Independent Producers.

AMOLAD was no sooner conceived in 1944 than it ran into the wartime rationing of Technicolor film stock and equipment. The Archers promptly devised another emblematic story, of 'a girl who wants to get to an island', but is prevented by a storm.[66] During that symbolic storm, she has fallen out of love with material success and in love with rural simplicity and impoverished aristocracy, rather as Peter falls in love with the voice of a girl from Boston during what he believes will be his last minutes of life. *IKWIG* was intended to be made in black and white, with its extensive exteriors and realistic special effects requirements, but in other respects it carried forward the innovative approach to structure and atmosphere which Powell and Pressburger had first adopted as a matter of necessity on *49th Parallel*.

That film had required Canadian locations, with a large and varied cast, at the height of the naval war in the North Atlantic. The solution involved extensive use of process photography and montage techniques, with doubles in long shots and model work. All of these were standard techniques of studio film production, but there was now a growing conviction that they could be used more systematically to make production faster, cheaper and more fluent. The prophet of this new approach, soon to be known as 'independent frame', was the art director on *49th Parallel*, David Rawnsley. Rawnsley became head of Rank's new research department and Powell chaired the steering group which oversaw this work, reporting enthusiastically on its potential in early 1945, and more fully in August, just ten days before *AMOLAD* began shooting.[67] Among the recommendations were:

The thorough and complete understanding of the Technique by everyone participating in the production from the initial stages to the final shooting.

The unqualified unification of effort by the Producer, Script Writer, Production Designer and the Directors of action, art, sound, music and colour, together with the production staff, and the various sub-departments, all of whom must work from the outset, closely together, as a group. ...

Above all, the report insisted, 'films are a visual art, and therefore, must be conceived visually.'

It is easy to imagine this emphasis on the visual worrying the writers especially among the Independent Producers.[68] But much of what was proposed also seems remarkably close to the integration of effort and effect which The Archers would now attempt. Not liking separate trick departments, Powell, 'decided magic and effects should be part of the art department, directly answerable to Uncle Alfred [Junge] and to me and to Jack Cardiff'; and close teamwork would characterise The Archers' most ambitious film to date.

Independent frame is all too often seen as a parochial British affair, born of post-war penny-pinching and bureaucracy, which produced only a handful of relatively mediocre films.[69] But it should be seen in the context of a widespread desire to integrate all the elements of film more organically – an impulse as apparent in Eisenstein's operatic *Ivan the Terrible* dyptich (1944–6), for which he acted as writer, director and designer, as in Hitchcock's first colour films, *Rope* (1948) and *Under Capricorn* (1949), with their attempt to create a claustrophobic intensity through seamless long takes. In this sense, *AMOLAD* might be considered one of the first films to embody the vision of independent frame.[70]

Colour

Producing an elaborate colour fantasy in 1945 involved making a crucial choice from a small group of cinematographers with Technicolor experience. Powell's first experience of colour had been on *The Thief of Bagdad*, photographed by the veteran Georges Périnal, and for The Archers' first venture in colour, *Blimp*, he turned to Périnal, whose exquisite photography served the period sequences well, although Powell

England in question on the night of a 1000 bomber raid on Germany

An airman's love letter to England: Peter in the blazing cockpit

Predestined lovers: Peter and June's first meeting on the beach

The Hoffmanesque
Conductor 71
demonstrating his
powers

Optical mastery:
Dr Reeves surveying
his patients by camera
obscura

Rehearsing a
rehearsal: the
Mechanicals in
*A Midsummer Night's
Dream*

Allegories of design:
framed between
The Dream and chess,
Dr Reeves takes on
Peter's case

A modern magus:
Roger Livesey as
Dr Reeves en route to
his role as guardian
angel

'A mixture of Piccadilly
Circus escalator and
St Paul's Cathedral':
Peter and Conductor
71 debating on the
stairway

'Be of good cheer':
John Bunyan hands
Dr Reeves over to the
Conductor, who has
'borrowed' his chess
book

The cases converge:
Peter conjured out of
his operation to brief
Dr Reeves

Wagner meets the
United Nations: the
heavenly amphitheatre

Levels of jurisdiction:
the court visits the
scene of Peter's earthly
'case'

'We've won': the rights
of the post-war couple
vindicated

The original release
poster

'I want! I want!' Engraving from *The Gates of Paradise*, William Blake, 1793

Blake's *Jacob's Ladder* (© copyright The British Museum)

Christina's vision: illustration from *The Pilgrim's Progress* (Bagster ed., anon.)

Alfred Junge designing the operating theatre

Junge's original design
for the 'Wing Section'

Bob waiting for Peter in
the reception scene as
filmed

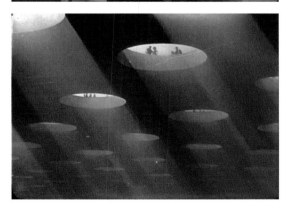

Windows into the
Piranesian Records
Section

Vincent Korda's influential futuristic design for *Things to Come* (1936)

A meeting with the heavenly C.O. in *A Guy Named Joe* (1944) with set decoration by Edwin B. Willis

The Heart of England (1943), an allegorical portrait of Richard Hillary by Eric Kennington

remained 'not satisfied with the modern episodes at all'.[71] Meanwhile, Erwin Hillier had photographed both of the intervening black-and-white films, rising to the challenge of their (very different) evocative landscapes and the technical difficulty of melding location, studio and process images. But Hillier had no experience of colour, then almost a separate craft, so Powell proposed that he share responsibility with the Technicolor specialist Jack Cardiff, who had not yet had a solo feature credit.

Hillier refused, so Cardiff got his chance to launch a remarkable career. He had already worked for The Archers on the second unit of *Blimp* – shooting the series of stuffed animal heads which mark Clive Candy's restless bachelor period between the Boer and Great wars – when Powell abruptly asked if he would shoot their next colour feature. With the film's delay, Cardiff went to work on Gabriel Pascal's *Caesar and Cleopatra* (another Independent Producers' project), before the summons came.

AMOLAD and *Black Narcissus*, for which Cardiff won an Academy Award, have become part of Technicolor's legend. The company had been founded by Herbert Kalmus in Boston in 1915 and an early version of the process was available from 1922, when DeMille used it for the Old Testament section of his *Ten Commandments*.[72] In 1928 Technicolor introduced its imbibition technique, using initially two negatives to record different colour values, which then controlled the density of two dyes – red and green – in the positive print. However, the arrival of this process coincided with that of synchronised sound, which also necessitated heavy investment by producers and caused its own technical problems, resulting in a delayed take-up of colour.

Technicolor added a third negative in 1932, which gave improved colour reproduction but required an even larger camera that now had to be 'blimped' to avoid interference with sound recording. Increased lighting was needed, and design, costume and make-up all required more attention. The whole process, including final release prints, raised the cost of production by up to a third – and its appeal to audiences was still unproven.[73] It was in this uncertain climate, in 1935, that Technicolor established a London branch; and one of the first recruits for training was Jack Cardiff, then an operator at Denham Studios. Cardiff thought his non-technical approach would disqualify him, but his interviewers apparently were impressed by his enthusiasm for painting.[74] Indeed the challenge facing Technicolor's early users, apart from its technical limitations, was how to move beyond the novelty stage of colour as decoration, and what the painter Paul Nash called 'naïve attempts at colour harmony', towards its fluent use in narrative, or even in new kinds of spectacle.[75]

The first films that Cardiff worked on were frankly devoted to displaying colour as exotic. However, the war diverted Technicolor into a range of specialised uses, for training and record films, that helped weaken the aesthetic dictatorship wielded by the formidable ex-wife of Technicolor's founder, Natalie Kalmus, who demanded a luridly chromatic palette, with flat, even lighting. Anything approaching chiaroscuro, or deliberate variation of exposure, was forbidden.[76] But on the feature documentary about North Atlantic convoys *Western Approaches* (Pat Jackson, 1944), Cardiff discovered that if he took off the blue filter normally used to 'correct' incandescent lighting, he could create artificial sunlight: 'I over-exposed the negative which bleached the grey sky into white, and instructed the Technicolor laboratories to correct the orange light by printing it much bluer and, hey presto, the overcast sky became a bright blue and the captain's face healthily sunlit.'[77] Such wartime experiences undoubtedly helped Technicolor emerge from its kindergarten stage, best suited to the display of exotic locations and 'colourful' stories. And in *AMOLAD* Cardiff was able to pursue his tonal experiments, as in the table-tennis scene which is interrupted by the heavenly Conductor, where he used a lemon rather than an amber filter to create 'the magical atmosphere the scene was meant to have'.[78]

AMOLAD also posed new challenges. It was to be a fantasy, with special effects creating Peter's 'highly organised hallucination' of heaven, but of a very different kind from either of the benchmark Technicolor fantasies, *The Wizard of Oz* or *The Thief of Bagdad* (closer, in fact, to Goldwyn's 1945 Danny Kaye vehicle *Wonder Man*). Here Cardiff's experience on commercials and on the demonstration film would prove invaluable. *Oz* had only required 'bracketing' monochrome at the beginning and end, but frequent cuts from colour to black-and-white stock would be jarring and make release prints physically fragile. Printing the monochrome scenes on colour stock – treating them as drastically reduced colour – was a good mechanical solution which also offered the advantage of controllable transitions (dissolves), and a monochrome that was tonally compatible with the full colour sequences. Powell dramatised the moment of decision in his memoir:

'What will three-strip without the three primary colours look like?' we
all wanted to know.
　'Sort of pearly,' said Jack vaguely.
　I looked at Alfred. 'Did you hear, Alfred? Open wide them
pearly gates!'[79]

If heaven would become 'pearly', as it has been traditionally in visual representation, colour represents the freshness and tangibility of the
everyday – an Arcadian beach, the archetypal English village and coun-
tryside – everything that Peter will lose if he submits to death. The
Conductor's famous joke about being 'starved for Technicolor up there',
apparently added in dubbing and delivered amid over-ripe rhododen-
drons, is both a dig at Technicolor and a witty reinforcement of the film's
anti-determinist philosophy. More dramatically, when Peter runs down
the stairway to escape back to consciousness, he literally regains colour.
Not until Antonioni's *Red Desert* (1964) or Tarkovsky's *Solaris* (1972)
would colour again signify 'life' so vividly.

Design
Alfred Junge, the German production designer, was the most experienced
of the core team responsible for *AMOLAD*. He had worked at the UFA studios with Paul Leni, famous for the fantastic *Waxworks*
(*Waxfigurenkabinett*, 1924), then with E. A. Dupont, accompanying him
to England after the international success of *Variety* (1925), and designing
the series of prestige films with which British International Pictures aimed
to raise domestic production standards in 1928-30. Thereafter he worked
for Paul Czinner, Alexander Korda and Hitchcock, before becoming head
of the art department at Gaumont-British and for MGM's major British
productions of the late 30s.
　Junge joined Powell and Pressburger on their second film,
Contraband (1940), a quirky thriller set in the Blitz, for which he created
some ingenious settings that drew on the subdued expressionism of his
work for Dupont. When he rejoined them on *Blimp*, there was a notice-
able architectural quality about the design – from the Turkish Bath in
which Clive begins his journey back through time, through the Berlin
scenes, and finally to Clive's 'lair'. In *A Canterbury Tale* and *IKWIG*, he
would prove equally adept at creating solid, yet atmospheric spaces, such
as the four-poster inn room where Sgt. Sweet wakes up in a vision of

'Merrie England'; or the Hebridean *ceildhe* where Joan realises there's more to life than marrying the boss.

AMOLAD would require some evocative architectural spaces like these: intimate in Dr Reeves's house, with its camera obscura and library; and stately in Lee Wood House's vast hall. Beyond these, it also needed a convincing vision of heaven, and of the giant moving stairway which would give the film its central motif – a twenty-foot wide 106-stair escalator (nicknamed 'Ethel' and driven by a 12 hp engine).[80] But any idea that there was a simple progression from script to screen is called into question by trying to trace the *visual* evolution of the all-important introduction to heaven. In Pressburger's draft this reads:

CLOAKROOM

For a moment we only see the cascading cloud of yellow fog. Then it blows away and the whole picture is filled out by a big, snow-white pair of wings. As we move back we realise we are in a kind of cloakroom. Behind the attendant's desk there are thousands of pairs of white wings packed in rows, reaching far back, so deep that we can't see the end of them. The windows are much deeper to let in more light, which comes from below, as if it would be below and not above. The shadows are in accordance with this.

The attendant is a sweet-looking girl in WAAF uniform. She is busy to pull off a kind of dust-sheet from a brand new pair of wings. There are other attendants and customers.

On the other side of the desk [as first of a queue] a man in RAF uniform is signing an enormous book. Behind him there are several doors with little glass panels.

Here heaven is still in colour, until the attendant touches Bob's eyelids and

From nowhere she produces a transparent veil-like something cut like a pair of glasses. We have a flash of colours through it as she removes it. … From here everything is black and white. …

Recalling Corinthians' 'through a glass, darkly', or even Conan Doyle's 'psychic spectacles', this provided an early rationale for the shift from colour to monochrome. But by the shooting script stage, it had been dropped. Heaven now simply is monochrome:

The fog, greyish, yellowish, dun-colour, swirls about, what colour it
has seems to be draining away, until shades of black and white are all
that remain. …
The black and white fog dissolves.
Through it appear hundreds of pairs of wings – white wings.

Scene 23 THE CLOAKROOM retains Pressburger's idea of light seeming to
come from below and the centrality of the heavenly ledger:

There are many windows and the light streams in through them from
below as if the sun were below instead of above as in our world.
There are ATTENDANTS and a desk with a great book.
Over the desk a sign: 'Airmen Section'.

The scene described has many Attendants, working behind the counter
and measuring new arrivals, with 'thousands of pairs of wings, parked in
rows, reaching far back'. A line of Airmen at the counter, 'men of all
nations', receive their wings before leaving through a door marked
'INSTRUCTORS', followed by the exchange between Bob and the WAAF
Angel, more or less as in the final film.

Missing, however, was the dynamic that is provided by different
nationalities entering the cloakroom, which is tersely noted in Powell's
handwriting on the reverse of the facing page:

Crane shot. Track back from wings to show counter and WAAFs.
Read sign. General impression of what is going on. Pan over to show
Bob waiting in foreground. New arrivals coming in.

Dramatically, this improves on the static conception of the scene, which
could only be animated by a 'reveal', then shot-reverse-shot construction
over the counter. Powell's notes quickly link the reception Angel with
Bob, waiting for his Captain, and introduce as a new focus of interest the
entrance. Through this comes a sequence of different national and class
stereotypes – a gesticulating Frenchman with a laconic Englishman; a
solitary harmonica player; the 'wide-eyed' (according to the script)
young pilot played by Richard Attenborough; a bustling American
bomber crew – rapidly establishing the film's underlying theme and
preparing for the national and period stereotypes of the climactic court

scene. This evokes the same sense of diverse people thrown together by the theatre of war that occurs in Humphrey Jennings's "*Fires Were Started* – " (1943) when a series of firemen enter the duty room one after another to the accompaniment of 'One Man Went to Mow' played on the piano.

However, the filmed and edited version of the scene is different again. It is played mainly on Bob; and now design makes an important contribution to establishing this Other World as futuristic and efficient. Instead of the counter, which appears in one of Junge's drawings as a large 'window' with curved corners, the two similarly styled doorways become dominant. The exit, seen first, has an automatic transparent sliding door which allows aircrew through carrying their wings, while the entrance is reached by an escalator, prefiguring the main celestial stairway. Similarly, the Reception Angel shows Bob the vast records department through a circular well; and a reverse shot (apparently graphic) reveals this as one of innumerable such wells. If this perspective seems Piranesian, the Other World's Cloakroom is distinctly modernist, recalling the celestial police court of Lang's *Liliom* (1933), or the future Everytown of Korda's *Things to Come*, with its eclectic mixture of Le Corbusier, the Bauhaus and Norman Bel Geddes.[81] Many downtrodden citizens of 1946 might be happy to work in this modern bureaucracy, as the angel pointedly reminds the upper-class Bob.

Such an evolution from first concept to realisation on screen is not uncommon in film-making; and it is likely that many had a say in it. The original motif of modernity versus tradition – will there be 'props or wings' in the Other World? – remains central, and is now wittily developed through dialogue, characterisation and especially design. But there were already signs of tension between Junge's innate realism and The Archers' growing appetite for fantasy – specifically in this scene a clash over Powell's introduction of a Coca-Cola machine into the heavenly Cloakroom.[82] Junge could achieve miracles of illusionism, as in the cathedral constructed in Stage 4 at Denham for *A Canterbury Tale*, but Powell recalled how, on *AMOLAD*, when he saw the same stage 'filled to overflowing with Alfred's giant rocks and vast stadium full of costumed people, my heart failed me. I thought I would never be able to get all this airborne'.

The problem here – if it is a problem – might be traced to the original conception of a heavenly tribunal. Junge's solution to this daunting challenge clearly harks back to the new scenography of the turn of the century. The sweeping staircase that leads to the heavenly tribunal's podium recalls Adolphe Appia's pioneering use of steps and platforms; while the rocky outcrops on which Reeves and his adversary perch recall versions of the mountain settings required in Wagner's *Die Walküre*. The podium is geometric modernist, like the Cloakroom, and the transparent table on which the rose with June's tear as 'evidence' sits (described as a 'slab' in the script) recalls the futuristic Perspex furniture of *Things to Come*. It is clear from the script that the large blocks of extras were intended to be used for an even wider variety of reaction shots, punctuating and underlining the opposing counsels' arguments, than survive in the film. Powell's annotations to the shooting script pose questions about the permutation of available angles and about the composition of the audience groups: 'Is the WAAF officer with Bob? Do we mix the sexes? Can they be on opposite sides of the gangway?'

The stairway connecting heaven and earth had been an early feature of the film's conception and 'moving stairs' are mentioned in Pressburger's notes on the role of music. The idea of flanking statues of the famous may well have come from (or itself suggested) the reference in the opening scene to where this world leaves off, 'or where it could leave off if we'd listened to Plato and Aristotle and Jesus'. The shooting script describes the escalator as

> enormously long and wide, neither the top nor the bottom are within sight. It looks like a mixture of Piccadilly Circus escalator and St Paul's Cathedral. It travels up swiftly into the clouds, while on each side, at intervals, are statues of the most famous people in the history of the world, some with their names, some with famous quotations. ... We see Plato, Socrates, Abraham Lincoln, Confucius, Julius Caesar (*Veni Vidi Vici*), King Solomon, Shakespeare, Mohammed, Alexander the Great (Legs), Michael Angelo, Moses, Benjamin Franklin, Chopin, Murillo, Swift, Rembrandt, Beethoven, etc.

The effect is to make the stairway less metaphysical and more didactic, and also to raise stylistic problems which had been successfully avoided by the modernist economy of earlier celestial scenes. And yet the statues were clearly important, at least to Powell, as a pantheon of human wisdom. A typed note survives, annotated by him, with a 'List of Statues on the Model Escalator' from which he chose (in order): Plato, Solomon,

Lincoln, Swift, Alexander, Homer, Beethoven, Chopin (and, written in, 'Capt. Scott RN'). In the end, only three statues are identified by the Conductor (Lincoln, Plato and Solomon) as he tries to tempt Peter before the hearing and we see Caesar, Chopin and Mohammad. The statues attracted some sharp criticism, especially in France. A hostile Jacques Brunius included 'statues of great men in plasticine' in his catalogue of the film's banalities; while André Bazin, in an otherwise favourable notice, could not 'excuse the horror of the plaster and plexiglass décor'.[83] On the other hand, with hindsight it is possible to see here the first steps towards a complex allegorised décor that would develop under Hein Heckroth's production design for The Archers' later films.

Meanwhile, Powell still greatly valued Junge's resource in solving such problems as the arrangement of the camera obscura scene and commissioning the escalator, and the hands-on approach that meant he 'designed and painted his own galaxies' for the film's opening. And Junge already had a following among British critics. Dilys Powell suggested that The Archers 'owe a great deal to the designs of Alfred Junge, whose sets for the celestial High Court and stratospheric escalator have at once the precision and the extravagance of hallucination'. But behind the scenes there was a growing tension between Junge's 'meticulous realism' and the 'suggestive atmosphere' for which Powell was aiming. A letter from Junge to the film's publicist referred to some dispute about his billing in publicity, and it is certainly surprising that his name does not appear among the credits in the 'book of the film' published in 1946.[84] Cardiff also found Junge dictatorial in how he expected his sets to be lit; and so, despite the Academy Awards that both won for Black Narcissus, Junge was dropped in the early stages of The Red Shoes.

The occasion for doing so was a desire to adopt the more painterly approach of Hein Heckroth, who had become part of Junge's team on AMOLAD, responsible for the Other World costumes. Heckroth had been a painter in Germany before becoming designer for the modern dance pioneer Kurt Jooss. His most famous project for Jooss was The Green Table (1932), a widely admired anti-war ballet based on Holbein's Dance of Death woodcuts with a strong Expressionist overlay, for which he produced elaborate masks, make-up, costumes and décor.[85]

If Heckroth was still in the background (Powell claimed not even to have known his name until two films later), Percy 'Poppa' Day was very much in the foreground. As Powell later wrote: 'The movies were created for Poppa Day [who] commanded respect and admiration from all who worked with him, because he *knew*.'[86] What Day knew was the whole bag of tricks now blandly termed 'special effects'. He was rumoured to have learned from Georges Méliès, the magician turned fantasy film-maker, who had pioneered multiple exposure and matte techniques at the turn of the century.[87] But it was as head of special effects at Denham that he came into his own, co-ordinating the effects required in colour for Korda's *Thief of Bagdad*. Above all he was a *bricoleur*, an experimenter who could rise to any occasion, and clearly a vital figure in the matte work required to make 'Ethel' a stairway through the galaxies, together with The Archers' other stalwart collaborator, the chief electrician in charge of lighting, Bill Wall.

Casting

Technology had already delayed *AMOLAD* by a year; now it was about to enter the fraught zone of casting. The Archers were fortunate both in the relationships they had already fostered with actors and in the climate of mid-1945 as the war ended. The easiest casting was Roger Livesey as Dr Reeves. They had already given Livesey the role of his lifetime in *Blimp* (although only after failing to get Olivier), and an attractive romantic lead part in *IKWIG*. Now Pressburger wrote the benign yet almost supernatural Dr Reeves especially with Livesey in mind, and he in turn grew a beard for this role as a modern magus.

Casting Raymond Massey as the opposing counsel was also easy. He had already appeared in *49th Parallel*, delivering the *coup de grâce* to the escaping Nazi lieutenant, and according to Powell he promptly 'cabled an enthusiastic affirmative: "For the Archers anytime, this world or the next"'.[88] Canadian-born Massey had been an established character actor since the early 30s on both sides of the Atlantic, turning his earnest, potentially sinister expression to advantage in parts ranging from Sherlock Holmes to Abraham Lincoln. The latter, as well as his role in *Things to Come* as the leader of the future society, also fitted him ideally to play the devil's advocate role in *AMOLAD* – an American revolutionary killed by British soldiers who can imagine little good coming from any future England.

Marius Goring had also seen service before with The Archers, playing a U-boat officer in their 1939 debut *The Spy in Black*. Most of his film roles to date had been 'foreign', possibly because he was well known to have fluent French and German (having studied in Paris, Germany and Austria), and because of his intense somewhat 'un-English' appearance. Goring, however, was impatient to play a romantic lead and wanted the part of Peter. The Archers insisted that it was the Conductor or nothing – and had Peter Ustinov in reserve, who had already appeared in '... *one of our aircraft is missing*'. According to Powell, they considered the possibility of the Conductor being German (perhaps a relic of his Hoffmannesque origins? – Powell still refers to him as 'the Collector' in his memoir), but decided this would be 'too much of a good thing' in the current political climate, and agreed that he should remain a French aristocrat executed in 1793. The resulting caricature evidently grated on some French viewers: Bazin referred to it as 'ridiculement galante', while conceding that it is 'vigoureusement animée'. In naturalistic or conventional realist terms, the Conductor is indeed highly exaggerated, from the accent to the lipstick, but the part is a vital one, carrying most of the film's humour, necessary to gild its message and its metaphysics, and also providing the essential link between the two dramatic worlds and a comic foil to Dr Reeves's similar role.

Even with the underpinning of Livesey, Massey and Goring in place, everything would still depend on the romantic couple, Peter and June. Peter is an artist, a dreamer and a squadron leader – a combination which had already been essayed in Asquith's and Rattigan's extremely popular *The Way to the Stars* by Michael Redgrave. Who else could make such a character attractive and believable in the context of *AMOLAD*'s fantasy? The rising Stewart Granger was briefly considered, but The Archers' first choice was David Niven, quintessentially English, yet an established Hollywood star before the war, with roles that had ranged from the swashbuckling (*The Charge of the Light Brigade*, 1936 and *The Prisoner of Zenda*, 1937) to the intrepid (*Dawn Patrol*, 1938), the debonair (*Bluebeard's Eighth Wife*, 1938) and the classic (Edgar in Wyler's *Wuthering Heights*, 1939). Niven had a military background and volunteered for service at the outbreak of war, appearing in only two war-related films for the following six years: Leslie Howard's *The First of the Few* (1942) and the semi-documentary *The Way Ahead* (1944), in which he trains a motley group of recruits. He proved to be both available and keen, although Rank would have to pay Sam Goldwyn handsomely for his services; and like many, he felt apprehensive about resuming his career after such a long break. The Archers' offer was a huge relief because although I had been disguising it from Primmie [his first wife] I was extremely nervous about my future. Six months is a long time for an actor to be out of business – six years is almost certain disaster. A whole new breed of stars had taken over the movie audiences and at thirty-five I had good reason to be worried. I was also highly apprehensive lest I had forgotten how to do it.[89]

Now Powell and Pressburger turned their attention to the remaining role, the air controller who falls for Peter by radio, before joining the struggle for his medical and spiritual salvation – intended for an unknown American actress who would be 'discovered' and propelled to fame by the film. David Selznick had famously publicised his search for a Scarlett O'Hara worthy of *Gone With the Wind* in 1939. Now The Archers would travel to Hollywood to conduct their own version of the same ritual, and do business with the same legendary Selznick. As Powell dramatised it in his memoir, the story is rich in symbolism – a tale of late imperial Hollywood. Powell and Pressburger travel in style across America, meeting first their hero Fritz Lang, then their near-contemporary, Alfred Hitchcock, the only British film-maker to have carved a secure reputation in Hollywood. News of their mission had spread. Knowing that they are 'looking for an all-American girl to co-star with David Niven ... every studio is grooming some floozy or other for the part'.

Hitchcock explained that they should have paid tribute first to Selznick, son-in-law of MGM's Louis B. Mayer. However, he has found them a suitable actress: 'sensible, pretty, could be the girl next door, can act, good voice, good legs'. Kim Hunter had appeared in a test Hitchcock was shooting for *Spellbound* and was already under contract to Selznick. Although only twenty-two, she had already appeared in five films, with stars of the calibre of Ginger Rogers and William Holden, having made her debut as the female lead in Val Lewton's *The Seventh Victim* (1943). Hunter duly reported the following day and was quickly accepted, not only for her 'chestnut hair and green eyes', but for the 'imagination and intelligence' evident in her speech. While waiting for the Technicolor camera to become available, she was pressed into service for an ingenious framing device intended to make *A Canterbury Tale* more attractive to American audiences. In this shortened version, the whole story of Sgt. Johnson's wartime adventures on the way to Canterbury is told in flashback to his American fiancée – an apt introduction to the culture of post-war Anglo-American relations.

There were many other smaller parts to be cast, drawing on personal and screen associations. Trubshaw, Peter's dead wireless-operator, intended as a comic foil with his flyer's slang and ready eye for angels, was played by Bob Coote, who had shared a house in Malibu with Niven (and the character, Malory in the script, renamed in tribute to Niven's larger-than-life former comrade in arms). Kathleen Byron, Trubshaw's first angelic attraction in the Cloakroom, had made her Archers' debut in *The Silver Fleet* (1943), and would go on to play their most convincing female roles in *Black Narcissus* (1947) and *The Small Back Room* (1948). Two cameo appearances in the Cloakroom scene would have had flying associations for the filmgoers of 1946: Bonar Colleano, captain of the Flying Fortress crew, had recently appeared as one of the American airmen who brashly move into the English aerodrome in *The Way to the Stars*; and Richard Attenborough was the lead in John Boulting's semi-documentary *Journey Together* (1944) for the RAF Film Unit.

Shooting

Much of *AMOLAD* would be created in the studio, pushing process techniques to new levels of sophistication in colour. There are only three actual exterior locations: the beach where Peter is washed up and meets June; the village, as surveyed by Dr Reeves's camera obscura; and the country roads that Reeves races around on his motorcycle, before sacrificing his earthly life on Peter's behalf. Of these, the beach is the most important, since it has to support the film's first establishment of an everyday earth, after the cosmic and heavenly openings, and its delicate balancing of myth and realistic melodrama.

The location chosen was Saunton Sands in North Devon, where Powell had first worked in Technicolor in autumn 1939, filming material for the genie scene of *The Thief of Bagdad* with Sabu and Rex Ingram. Now, the day that the war finally ended was also *AMOLAD*'s first day of shooting, with the once-idyllic beach showing signs of its use as a gunnery range. The scene on that first day is vividly recorded, both in publicity pictures and in Powell's own account.[90] Seeing that the tide would move quickly, he urged on the crew and cast to squeeze in as many set-ups as possible, from Peter's bobbing in the water to his walk out of the sea, discarding clothes and playing with his shadow. Then the 'Keep Out' sign – Alfred Junge was present for this first day, acting as hands-on art director – and the shepherd boy, naked to tease out the idea that this Arcadian scene could be the Other World, until a Mosquito swoops low to tell Peter that he's still in this world.

Powell looked at the published photographs from that day when writing his memoir, and it is easy to understand the emotions they stirred. Cardiff and Powell, both in sweaters, are actively choosing angles and lining up shots. Junge, in beret and overcoat, is a benign, avuncular figure. And the whole crew is seen queuing for an open-air lunch. The image is casual, vigorous, egalitarian, co-operative: an idealistic microcosm of the post-war world just beginning. Turn the page, and we are back at Denham, where the studio shoot began on 24 August. Now everyone is in suit and tie; and in contrast to the unblimped exterior camera, the studio Technicolor camera is a massive box, dwarfing its operators.

The beginning of studio work was marked by another milestone, this time a personal one for Powell, whose first son Kevin was born that day. Nothing, however, interfered with this long-planned production, which Powell recalled as 'a very happy film from start to finish'. Kim Hunter had been warned by Livesey that 'Micky can be a beast', confirming Powell's reputation for driving his collaborators hard, but her experience was entirely happy. So was Jack Cardiff's:

> Michael was a cameraman's dream. He nearly always accepted any ideas I put forward with enthusiastic support. Like all good minds he

Powell with Jack Cardiff on the first day's shooting at Saunton Sands

possessed a nervous vitality. He hardly ever just walked; quite often he leapt, or took great strides. If a problem arose, he would cradle his arms, ponder deeply for a few moments then pronounce his decision with utter finality – before leaping away.[91]

With many crew members well used to working together – although the schedule meant that many actors never actually met each other on set[92] – the twelve-week shoot finished a week early.

Two other key contributors to *AMOLAD* played their parts as shooting proceeded. Reginald Mills was editing his first film for The Archers, following in the footsteps of John Seabourne, who had also acted as an assistant director but was now forced by ill-health to retire. David Lean had edited two of their films, before starting to direct; and Mills had long been his assistant. He would stay with The Archers until the end of their partnership, later forming an equally long relationship with Joseph Losey.

However infuriating the punctual Pressburger found his erratic time keeping, they had a common love of music and worked closely together, since Pressburger was actively involved in editing after Powell took sole charge of the shoot. Despite the complexity of the process work on *AMOLAD*, Mills had a rough cut ready to view five days after the end of shooting.

54 Powell beneath the technicolor camera, with members of the crew, including Christopher Challis (far right) and Cardiff (third right)

Music

This was the point at which the last member of the creative team could go to work. 'Allan Gray' was the professional name used by Josef Zmigrod, a Polish-born composer whose career had followed a similar pattern to that of Pressburger. Having started at UFA – on a film that Pressburger also worked on, *Emil and the Detectives* (1931) – Gray moved to France and then England, where he found work through Korda, and again wrote the music for a film that Pressburger co-scripted, *The Challenge* (1938). Powell and Pressburger had been distinctly fortunate in the composers provided for their first films – Miklos Rosza for *Spy in Black* and Richard Addinsell for *Contraband* (1940). On *49th Parallel* they had persuaded no less a composer than Ralph Vaughan Williams to write his first film score. For *Blimp*, which required period quotation and pastiche, they turned to Gray, who would work on the next six films.

Of the two partners, Pressburger was the more actively musical: he had played the violin when young and later amassed a vast collection of classical recordings, listing Brahms as his favourite composer in 1943.[93] His preliminary notes on the placing of music in *AMOLAD* show a sophisticated understanding of the interplay of music, speech and natural sound in film; and a contemporary article on film music praises precisely this achievement:

> After a powerful opening (for the titles), the music which accompanied the first scenes of the Universe, the Planets, and Earth, and finally the locale of the first meeting with the main character ... is so designed that it fitted a commentary heard over these shots without ever clashing; it did not need fading in and out, but subtly amplified and sustained the narrator's story.[94]

Powell also brought his own enthusiasms and boldness to the music of his films. The last reel of *The Edge of the World* (1937) had featured one of the longest continuous passages hitherto recorded for a British film. And one of only two illustrations in his first volume of memoirs is Gray's 'stairway' theme, reproduced in the music score which he praises.

Allan Gray is not normally listed among the composers who made the 40s a golden age of film-music collaboration in Britain, but his contribution to *AMOLAD* was surely even greater than Powell recognised. For in addition to the eerie stairway motif, which suggests something as modern as

Bartok in its atonality rather than the merely conventional chromaticism of much film scoring, there is an equally effective minimal figure of just two high alternating chords, also on solo piano, for the first heaven scene, as Bob waits vainly for Peter. This is punctuated by a solo harmonica – a distinctive wartime timbre – accompanying Attenborough's entrance, and a bustling big band fanfare announcing the American bomber crew, before it culminates in the heavenly 'alarm', a high-register percussive tremolo with what sounds like harp, xylophone and other percussion.

There are many other passages of deft orchestration – a spectral electric organ accompanies Peter's awakening on the foreshore; while a florid pipe organ flourish opens onto the heavenly amphitheatre – and much ingenious internal referencing of motifs, such as the five note 'fate' figure heard over the main title, which recurs at crucial moments. There are also echoes of many composers, ranging from Saint-Saens and Vaughan Williams to the 'rose' motif of Strauss's *Der Rosenkavalier*, all serving to recall Gray's cosmopolitan background – he had studied with Arnold Schoenberg in Vienna – even if these are interspersed with passages as seemingly banal as the 'rhododendron' music accompanying the Conductor's first materialisation on earth (or is this deliberately ironic?). At its best, the music of *AMOLAD* is more than conventionally evocative: it underscores important parts of the film's meaning. The alternating chords that mark celestial time take their pulse from the moving hands of the heavenly clock, and their lack of tonal resolution conveys the paradox of 'timeless time'. Likewise, the repeated figure of the staircase theme, raised by a semitone each time, creates a strong sense of inexorability – the blind 'law' that Peter is challenging. And in the Lee Wood House scene already discussed, the segue from Mendelssohn's *Midsummer Night's Dream* music to the sinister stairway theme, justified by a change from gramophone to 'live' source, offers a rare example of true audiovisual montage, in which the film's poetic juxtaposition of two worlds, or two aspects of the same world, is made manifest.

3

. . . .

RESPONSES

I began to dream of other methods, new aerial adventures.

Paul Nash[95]

The Battle of Leicester Square
Of all The Archers' films, *AMOLAD* undoubtedly had the most presti-
gious launch. By the time it was chosen for a Royal Command Film
Performance in aid of charity in late 1946, their next project, *Black
Narcissus*, was already in post-production. This was not the first 'command performance' – that had been for Queen Victoria in April 1896,
followed by many other royal cinema occasions – but an equivalent to the
established Royal Command theatre and variety performances was considered an important 'honour' by the perennially status-conscious film
trade.[96] Originally planned for 1939, then postponed when war broke out,
it would now take place in a climate of patriotic emotion mixed with economic and political anxiety.

The selection committee, which included Arthur Rank, as
president of the Producers Association, and a representative of 'the
American film industry', as well as distribution and exhibition worthies,
duly viewed a range of British and American films submitted before
choosing *AMOLAD*. The committee's press announcement revealed only
that 'it deals with an unusual subject in a most unusual way', while the
Kinematograph Weekly columnist reflected general euphoria and
mounting anticipation:

> I have no first-hand knowledge of the film, which, of course, has not
> yet been shown.
>
> I do know one man who saw it at a sneak preview, and he
> reported that it was a picture of most unusual quality, handling a highly
> original theme in a provocative and imaginative way. In addition, it has
> big star values – David Niven heads the cast – and all the indications are
> that it is a film which will set millions talking. Meanwhile, the whole
> Trade will give the Archers a pat on the back on their important
> achievement.

Despite the strenuous implication that a British film's selection was not inevitable, any alternative would have been little short of scandalous while American films continued to dominate British screens without British films receiving equivalent US distribution.[97] The screening, however, was to be followed by 'an hour's stage show contributed by all the leading British films stars, and by a number of American stars who will fly specially from Hollywood for the occasion'.

The result, on Friday 1 November, was an enthusiastic crowd of between 7,000 and 10,000 which thronged Leicester Square to catch a glimpse of the King and Queen, with Princesses Elizabeth and Margaret, and some thirty stars, led by Ray Milland, Joan Bennett, Maria Montez and Pat O'Brien, and from Britain, Will Hay, Margaret Lockwood, Valerie Hobson, Stewart Granger and Michael Redgrave. In the next day's papers, it became 'The Battle of Leicester Square', with the King reported as saying 'I thought we might be casualties ourselves.' Celebrities had to fight their way through – two who had a hard struggle were Powell and the Prime Minister, Clement Atlee – and a hundred minor casualties were claimed. Amid the inevitable bickering over responsibility some sense of national pride can be discerned. The *Daily Herald* quoted Pat O'Brien admitting, 'Hollywood has never seen anything like this.' Target receipts for charity were duly exceeded (ticket prices began at 10s 6d, ranging up to twenty-five guineas); and as a special concession to post-war austerity ('because of laundry difficulties'), the King gave permission for men to attend in lounge suits. Even if *AMOLAD* itself offered little scope for fashion display, the Royal performance did, and the dresses worn by female stars were enthusiastically previewed.[98]

The stage show which followed the film gallantly tried to bridge the gap between Hollywood and Britain by drawing heavily on English-born stars. Marius Goring appeared first, in his Conductor 71 costume, with a fragment of early Keystone comedy, followed by Will Hay introducing an extract from Chaplin's *The Champ*; and later Ray Milland (also English-born) introduced scenes from the previous year's Academy Award winning *The Lost Week-End*, while Bud Flanagan humorously presented Maria Montez, known as the 'Queen of Technicolor'. However, there was criticism in the trade press of how speedily seventeen British stars were paraded across the stage, as evidence of the recent 'progress of British films'.

The background to this tension was a long-awaited visit to Britain by Eric Johnston, head of the Motion Pictures Producers and Distributors Association, to discuss the framing of a new Quota Act with the Chancellor of the Exchequer. Hollywood was known to be pressing for 'free trade', meaning an end to the requirement that UK exhibitors and distributors handle a fixed minimum proportion of domestic films. Against this, British producers, led by Rank, complained that few of their films could gain effective access to the American market. Even Olivier's acclaimed *Henry V*, singled out by Johnston for praise, had not been widely shown. Johnston's visit to Britain had already been postponed several times because of a long-running strike in Hollywood – he was quoted as admiring the British industry's more conciliatory labour relations – and in the following year, as the economic crisis worsened, a new Chancellor would impose a massive 75 per cent tax on the estimated earnings of imported films to conserve dollars, thus precipitating a full-scale Hollywood boycott of Britain. But this lay in the future as *AMOLAD* began its delayed bid to conquer the British imagination and box-office.

'Well, they've done it'
Much has been made of a long-standing native critical hostility towards Powell and Pressburger, reaching its climax in the vitriolic response to Powell's much later *Peeping Tom*. Contemporary reviewers' responses to *AMOLAD*, however, were generally positive, with only a minority of outright opponents. The main trade reviews were among the most enthusiastic, trumpeting the film's 'brilliant production qualities ... masterly use of colour, and remarkable blend of inventiveness and artistry' (*Today's Cinema*, 6 November 1946); and hailing it as a 'brilliantly conceived modern phantasmagoria, deftly executed in Technicolor ... its blend of ethereal fantasy and down-to-earth pathology and romance is superb' (*Kinematograph Weekly*, 7 November). Most of the popular dailies were equally favourable, with Leonard Mosley in the *Daily Express* identifying the pre-trial visit to the operating room as the point at which 'there was a sort of click inside me, and I said to my wife, "Well, they've done it."'

The main criticism, among these superlatives, was of the arguments against Britain's imperial record given to Abraham Farlan. For *Today's Cinema*, 'it is not to the picture's credit that it completely fails to give an answer to the Bostonian's bitter political arraignment.' However,

Kinematograph Weekly noted that 'some may take umbrage at the anti-British feeling shown during the trial scenes, but the majority of Britons will, we feel sure, display stout skins.' The same notice linked the film with the current trade imbalance:

> Now it is up to the Yanks, to whom it so consistently and gracefully panders. It is the complete answer to those who have been constantly bellowing for something different. It is a showman's proposition, and British at that!

Concern about the film's 'anti-British' stance appeared most Blimpishly in the *Daily Graphic* on 2 November:

> There will be widespread indignation at the choice for the first Royal Film Performance last night of a picture which might have been made specially to appeal to isolationist and anti-British sentiment in the United States. ... Old feuds, old grudges, old hatreds are revived in one scene of this film in a manner which is entirely unnecessary. ... Ancient charges against British 'Imperialism' which, for the most part, never had any real substance, are paraded – and no defence is offered.

This may seem unsophisticated, out of step with the film's self-definition as 'a stratospheric joke', yet the *Graphic*'s dour insistence that the film failed to refute charges against British imperialism also goes to the heart of a political debate or *negotiation*, of which the film was effectively a part. Like the right-wing pamphleteers, the Robsons, of whom more later, it takes the film seriously – even if, in doing so, it misreads the intended message.

For a number of broadsheet reviewers, *AMOLAD* amounted to a vindication of what The Archers had long promised. Campbell Dixon, in the *Daily Telegraph*, found it 'more plausible than *A Canterbury Tale* and less irritating than *Colonel Blimp*. In fact for the first time these clever collaborators have achieved charm' (2 November). Alexander Shaw went further in *The Spectator*, having 'not been a great admirer of their work':

> All these films had a certain distinction but there was always a baffling obstacle between intention and achievement. Now the fog has cleared, the maturing period is over. Powell and Pressburger have escaped

from their cage and stretched their cinematic legs. The dazzling result is worth all the growing pains.

For all his praise, Shaw concludes that 'finally [it] isn't about anything in particular unless Love Conquers All can be considered to be something'. He insists that his comment is not intended to denigrate 'a film which is an absorbing cinematic *tour de force*', but there remains the implied criticism that characterises much English response to 'art for art's sake' and modernism from the late nineteenth century onwards, often cloaked in xenophobia or anti-effeminacy.[99] The only unqualified contemporary defence of the film that I have found appeared in the British Film Institute's *Monthly Film Bulletin*. Signed 'RWD', this distinguishes 'those who like "down-to-earth" or matter-of-fact subjects' from 'those ... to whom fantasy and beauty and allegory appeal'. Only the latter will find 'this bold and imaginative *tour de force* ... fascinating'. The human characters other than Dr Reeves, it is suggested, are 'deliberately colourless', as if to underline their timelessness; and, in terms that echo its own 'metaphysical' wit, the film's success is defined as

> conveying an impression of a facet of eternity – an eternity in which even two lovers matter and yet nothing matters at all in comparison with an ultimate which is never revealed. In short, a brilliant experiment which will probably be enjoyed by many and appreciated only by a few.

This short review indicates that at least some viewers in 1946 – perhaps more than we will ever know – were sympathetic to the allegorical and self-referential fantasy proposed by *AMOLAD*.

Many reviewers, however, were clearly uncertain about how to pass their normal authoritative judgment. C. A. Lejeune, the respected *Observer* critic, mocked the film's tissue of literary quotations before settling for the complaint 'that it leaves us in grave doubts whether it is intended to be serious or gay'. Lejeune's counterpart at the *Sunday Times*, Dilys Powell, reached a nuanced version of the same ambivalent conclusion, finding that a melodramatic situation and novelettish characters rendered its central problem 'trivial' (3 November).

This leads to the influential group of periodical reviewers, mainly on the left, who took strong exception to the film's rejection of realism.

For Richard Winnington (*News Chronicle*), 'essential realism' is the 'true business of the British movie' (8 November); for Humphrey Swingler, as we have seen, *AMOLAD* contributed nothing to the 'tradition of solid native skill'; and for Frederic Mullally (*Tribune*), already hostile to Rank's ambitions, it lacked a 'dramatic link with real life people and their problems'. Mullally perhaps spoke for all of these when he claimed that 'fantasy is barren and meretricious unless used to convey a serious message' (8 November). By coincidence, a British film released the week after *AMOLAD* provided an object lesson for these critics in what British filmmakers should be doing. Winnington even referred to 'last week's pretensions', before discussing Peter Ustinov's *School for Secrets*, a tale of the scientists who invented radar. This affectionate account of a group of boffins thrown together by war work was welcomed as 'an essay in "Britishness"' and praised for walking a tightrope between overdrawn eccentricity and realistic character portrayal. Lejeune was equally enthusiastic: 'what is really interesting in the film is not the information [about radar] but the intuition. ... What Mr Ustinov has done so excellently is to gather together ... a collection of scientists who might have been types, but are individuals' (*Observer,* 10 November). For these reviewers, *School for Secrets* was everything that *AMOLAD* was not: properly 'British', unpretentious in portraying the exceptional, and paying due regard to the representation of character and relationship.

Some thirty years later, in a pioneering study of British critical discourse, John Ellis concluded that contemporary reviewers' responses to *AMOLAD* almost all reveal a 'yes, but ...' pattern, hinging on the 'moral force' that is invested in realism, and betraying different degrees of resentment at 'being held separate from the immediate emotional involvement that they expect from a narrative fiction film'.[100] Returning to these reviews does not contradict Ellis's analysis, but it shows that *AMOLAD* did benefit, at least initially, from the prestige of its royal launch; that there was a considerable spectrum of approval, some of it unqualified; and that there were concerns other than aesthetic, notably about its 'argument'.

Reviving The Archers
When a non-journalistic tradition of film criticism emerged in Britain after the Second World War, led by the young critics and future filmmakers who founded *Sequence* magazine at Oxford, it found invention,

'expression' (a key term) and 'emotional truth' in British films as various
as *Henry V*, *Brief Encounter*, *Odd Man Out*, *Men of Two Worlds* and *Hue
and Cry*, while citing Ford's *My Darling Clementine* as a 'supreme example' of transforming conventional material. But in Powell (the joint credit
is ignored in *Sequence*'s proto-auteurism) it could see only 'hokum',
'pompous narrative devices' and '*kitsch*', while feeling that he 'remains
potentially one of the most interesting British directors'.[101] *AMOLAD*,
however, was dismissed in a single phrase as 'a very arid and pretentious
work'; and throughout the rest of the 40s, continuing into the 50s and 60s,
the critical reputation of The Archers, and then of Powell and
Pressburger separately, continued to decline.

It was not until the mid-60s, after a new critical avant-garde had
emerged in Britain around *Movie*, that the case of Powell would be re-
opened. Raymond Durgnat's outstanding 1965 essay laid the
groundwork for most subsequent appreciation of Powell (with
Pressburger minimally acknowledged), sketching a vivid ideological pro-
file to match the stylistic trajectory of Powell's career from *The Thief of
Bagdad* to *Peeping Tom*. Here Durgnat argued for the coherence of
AMOLAD in terms of its 'explicit ideological position ... [a] High Tory
moral':

> The film then ceases to be an assemblage of technical effects and
> metaphysical tags: whatever its weaknesses (which themselves
> indicate the spirit of its time and class) it has a consistent theme and
> 'body', and its various episodes and ingredients appear as spokes
> radiating from a central hub ... his critics ... didn't see that the film
> was as political as *The Life and Death of Colonel Blimp*.[102]

If this claim now seems obvious, it is an indication of how low
Powell–Pressburger's reputation and visibility had sunk by the mid-60s,
with only *Peeping Tom* enjoying a shadowy *film maudit* reputation. And
despite Durgnat's advocacy, followed by Kevin Gough-Yates's published
interviews and retrospectives in the early 70s, the films remained little
seen or discussed until the end of that decade, when restorations and retrospectives began to build a body of interest and a demand for new
interpretations.[103]

Taking its cue from Powell's proclaimed hostility towards naturalism, much of this new consensus was built around the idea of a

counter-tradition, challenging British realism and flaunting a commitment to art and the values of Romanticism and its twentieth-century descendants, Expressionism and Surrealism.[104] The Archers' alleged deviance and their condemnation were seen positively, as evidence of their standing outside the despised tradition of 'academic' realism. Unlike such contemporaries as Lean, their reputations grew and they became the prototype of a modern auteur – multiple (as a partnership), European in orientation, eclectic in style and source material.

The canonisation of Powell and Pressburger in auteur terms has directed attention to recurrent thematic and formal motifs in their work, all of which can be identified in *AMOLAD* and have structured how the film is now widely understood, namely:

(a) A concern with nationality and cultural identity (Durgnat's 'explicit ideological position' and 'consistent theme') which was evident as early as *Edge of the World* and *The Spy in Black*, reaching its climax in *AMOLAD* with a full-scale debate about what 'England' meant at the end of the Second World War, challenged from outside, now by its ally, America, rather than by its enemy, Nazi Germany.

(b) The artist as outsider – a motif of Romantic pessimism identified in an important essay by Thomas Elsaesser on *The Tales of Hoffmann* – is represented in *AMOLAD* by Peter as a poet-turned-pilot, cut short in his development.[105] So too are the related themes of the artist as a rebel against conformity and manipulation; and of the gulf between the space of imagination/performance and the everyday world. Peter, like later Powell–Pressburger heroes, refuses to accept a bureaucratic decision, and creates a theatre of his own imagination, even more spectacular than the hallucinatory stages of *The Red Shoes* or *The Tales of Hoffmann*.

(c) Specularity – the concern with vision and visual re-presentation – was noted by Durgnat, and later amplified by Ellis, as a recurrent motif in Powell–Pressburger's films. In Ellis's analysis of *AMOLAD*, an analysis of the 'disjunctions' between documentary and fictional modes is shown to structure much of the film – not only such spectacular moments as the Conductor's reference to Technicolor, the camera obscura and the giant eyelid closing, but also a passage such as the table-tennis game, shown in rapid pans and then frozen. Specularity had become a key to unlocking and interlocking the film's many themes by 1991, when it featured prominently in Marcia Landy's discussion.[106]

Analysing the corpus of Powell or 'Powell–Pressburger' from an auteur standpoint has laid to rest a long-standing charge of the erratic pursuit of effect or, in Durgnat's phrase, the 'mindless eye'. It has demonstrated an impressive consistency across a large body of work, relating theme to style, and revealing the evolution (if not the sources) of many recurrent motifs. At the same time, like all auteur scholarship, it has shed little light on working contexts or practices – on the relationship between the film-makers and with their colleagues and materials. It has perhaps discouraged different kinds of interpretation which would explore how a film's discourses interact with other discourses, to create meanings not necessarily intended or indeed foreseen by its authors. Commercial cinema, after all, is much less a form of private, or even purely artistic, utterance than most 'arts'; and so it unavoidably acts as a 'medium', encoding and transmitting many messages. It is to some of these extra-filmic discourses that I now turn.

Affairs of State
AMOLAD struck some reviewers as untimely or miscalculated in its portrayal of Anglo-American relations. But what of those who took it seriously as political propaganda? And what indeed can we make of its politics, however well disguised as a 'joke', in the tradition of Swift or Voltaire?

A minor curiosity of Powell–Pressburger scholarship is the vitriolic criticism of 'the Robsons', whose fanatical indictment of The Archers' wartime films has often been taken to stand for a wider disquiet. E. W. and M. M. Robson self-published a pamphlet in 1944 entitled *The Shame and Disgrace of Colonel Blimp*, in which they 'exposed' Powell and Pressburger's insidious undermining of the war effort by attributing common sense to the German character, Theo Kretchmar-Schuldorff, and, allegedly, pouring scorn on all things English. For the Robsons, any attempt to distinguish Nazis from Germans, or to criticise Britons, especially those in authority, was effectively crypto-fascism, as they continued to claim in a 1947 book:

Now, at last, the mask is off. Now it is safe to do openly in *A Matter of Life and Death* what could only be done slyly and covertly in *Blimp* and *49th Parallel*. Now it is safe to attempt to do during peace what the Goebbels–Hitler–Himmler crew failed to do during the war – bash the British in the sight of our Allies and create mischief between us and the Americans.[107]

To put this assault in context, it comes after equally unbridled accusations against Michael Balcon, Arthur Rank and Anthony Asquith, with the latter accused of wallowing in depravity akin to 'the last stages of dissolution and disruption of the Roman Empire' – and this in *Fanny By Gaslight*! The Robsons's main complaint about *AMOLAD* was, inevitably, that it mocked all things 'British'; and this they attributed, with more than a suggestion of anti-Semitism, to 'the Central European mind' which, for instance, 'cannot grasp what is behind and beneath the surface of cricket'. Somewhat bizarrely for such right-wing ideologues the Robsons invoke Freud and the idea of 'the sub-conscious [disguising] its immoral or anti-social impulse by clothing itself with all manner of symbols or convenient alibis'. Thus, the whole heavenly apparatus is seen as an elaborate subterfuge to trick 'plain, ordinary people like you and me' into accepting 'the naked German-Nazi-Fascist philosophy which is about to be rammed down your throat'.

What is perhaps most surprising is that this nonsense has continued to be quoted in almost all studies of The Archers, reaching a much wider audience than the Robsons can ever have expected.[108] However, this is not to deny *AMOLAD* any political intention. A more interesting insight into its contemporary interpretation emerges from a review published in the Soviet Union in 1947, under the title 'Mysticism and Politics', which had been translated and annotated by the British Embassy in Moscow for transmission to the Foreign Office.[109] The writer reports having seen the film in London, 'where it caused no small sensation', due to its 'symbolical and significant title [and] its extremely eccentric and unusual subject'. However, neither the 'mystical-philosophical sauce' nor profound deliberations on the all-conquering power of the 'simple love of simple people' can disguise its 'unequivocal ... political trend'.

Narrating the film in some detail, the Soviet writer enlarges on Reeves's and Farlan's negative characterisations of each other's culture – the British marked by 'spiritual poverty ... decadence and degeneration' and the American by 'legalised hypocrisy, which conceals the unlawful egotism of the dominating classes' – before observing that 'the producers have not succeeded in glossing over ... the real and earthly contradictions between America and Britain'. They attempt to overcome these by arguing that it would be 'better to find a happy ending, for the old and the new world to forget past wranglings, i.e. for Britain and America to throw themselves into each other's arms'; and in this, the 'echo is clearly heard of another speech ... made by Mr Churchill in Fulton, which has left a sombre trace on Britain's foreign policy'. Churchill's speech at Fulton, Missouri, on 5 March 1946 had famously proclaimed that 'an iron curtain has descended across the Continent' and called for 'a fraternal association of the English speaking peoples', based on a 'special relationship between the British Commonwealth and the United States'. Although out of office as Prime Minister, Churchill still had great prestige, especially in America, and the speech is now generally believed to have had Truman's tacit support as a 'trial balloon for a firmer policy towards the USSR'.[110]

Brushing aside any question of 'philosophical or theological depth', the Soviet commentator reads the film as aiming to 'instill in the spectator the idea that the creation of a bloc consisting of Britain and America is now a matter of life and death', adding that this deduction will follow easily from glancing at 'the headlines of articles in British daily papers and respectable weeklies'. The review's main conclusion is heavily marked in the Foreign Office copy; and a covering note from the British Minister in Moscow, Frank Roberts, describes it as 'an extreme example of the lengths to which Soviet propaganda can go in misrepresentation, or perhaps in genuine misunderstanding'. He then adds: 'Of course, the article fits beautifully into the main current propaganda theme of the Anglo-American bloc', before suggesting that the film's producers 'would be surprised to learn ... what their motives were'. In the tense context of 1946–7, this assumption seems naïve, or disingenuous. It was precisely British policy to argue for a continuation of the close wartime alliance between Britain and America, sometimes referred to as 'Anglo-America'; and considerable frustration was felt that Roosevelt insisted on trying to avoid giving Stalin the impression of Atlantic 'ganging up' against the USSR. Hence the attempt to tie his successor Truman into a 'firmer' stance. That the film indeed 'fits beautifully' into this British propaganda theme is therefore unlikely to be by chance, especially since much of the trial's mechanics are directed towards quelling American hostility towards British imperialism and effectively implementing Churchill's policy of 'mixing up' British and American affairs.

We do not know if Powell and Pressburger received any political briefing, but it is worth quoting two documents of the period which they could have seen. One is a Foreign Office official's report on American public opinion in the summer of 1945, which believed

> The future of the world depended on two 'colossi', the Soviet Union and the United States. Britain was so weakened economically by war and her Commonwealth so scattered that she could almost be overlooked in American policy.

> Britain was 'as full of tricks as a monkey' and would probably outsmart the United States and its inept State department in commercial and political dealings, thus managing to drag Americans into things that were not in their interest.[111]

A confidential memo from the Washington Embassy in November 1945 sought to translate these concerns into 'a positive line', showing 'that in peace as in war, we are able, tough, determined and dependable'; that the Commonwealth and Empire will be a beacon of stability 'in a confused world'; and, crucially, 'that we seek a close working partnership with the United States'.[112] Whether or not The Archers received any fresh briefing when they returned to the *AMOLAD* project in 1945, the film clearly follows the 'line' that Britain and the US must set past differences aside and forge a new relationship – symbolised by an American jury entrusting June to Peter's lifetime care.

As America unveiled the 'European Recovery Programme', better known as the Marshall Plan, following the Secretary of State's speech in June 1947, *AMOLAD* was playing its part in Britain's diplomatic strategy, opening in Paris, Rome, Zurich, Budapest, Johannesburg and many more capitals, no doubt with invited first-night audiences of opinion-leaders. The Russian report, published in May, was itself part of the new Soviet propaganda line which replaced wartime solidarity with a calculated attack on America's post-war role. In film terms, this continued with what would be Eisenstein's last article, 'Purveyors of Spiritual Poison', a polemic against recent American cinema published in *Sight and Sound*, followed by films such as *The Russian Question* (Romm, 1948) and

Meeting on the Elbe (Alexandrov, 1949).[113] Hollywood duly responded with Wellman's *The Iron Curtain* (1948) and the luridly titled *I Married a Communist* (Stevenson, 1949). *AMOLAD* thus inescapably belongs to the first phase of cinema's remobilisation in the Cold War.

Life, Love and Law

An aspect of *AMOLAD* which invites much more attention than it has received is the climactic trial itself. Instead of continuing to regard this as a somewhat tiresome legacy of the project's origin as a 'commission', as Powell indicated ('the MoI wanted this'), should we not follow Bazin's judgment that 'the long sequence of the heavenly trial … is worthy of inclusion in future anthologies of British cinema'? The film in fact can be seen to turn upon a significant play on words: Peter's medical *case* becomes, for him and for us, a legal *case*. The legal metaphors that we habitually use in medical situations – the patient is winning his fight / holding his own; doctors as arbiters of life and death, etc. – are here made literal in the parallel between the medical and legal 'cases'. So, if Peter's medical case turns out to be based on clinical practice, can any equivalent be found for the heavenly tribunal?

Unusual jurisdictional situations were certainly in the public consciousness in 1945–6. The Nuremberg trials of German leaders before a four-power tribunal began in November 1945; and many other indictments of collaborators and traitors in occupied countries had put issues of personal responsibility and 'national interest' on the legal agenda. Moves were under way to create a new global forum, replacing the pre-war League of Nations, which led to the United Nations Charter being drawn up at a conference in San Francisco in April–June 1945 and the UN coming into existence formally in October of that year, with provision for an International Court of Justice. These we may regard as the real-world correlates for the film's 'appeal court' in which all nations are represented – a very different conception indeed from the traditional denationalised 'last judgment' court of Revelation. But despite its spectacular scale, is this more than a convenient, or conventional way, to dramatise contending positions – an inflated version of the familiar dramatist's maxim, 'if in doubt, take the story to court'?

Drawing on recent critical legal studies, I think we can see it in a more subtle and imaginative light. *AMOLAD*'s appeal court is a fiction based on what Peter Goodrich has identified as the 'minor jurisprudences', such as 'ecclesiastical courts, civilian courts, courts of conscience, courts of equity ... of merchants, of forests, of harvests, of circuses, of fairs, of statuses, of women, of aliens', etc.[114] He invokes Deleuze and Guattari (writing about minor literature) to help define how these 'discarded traditions' relate to established law: 'where one believed there was the law, there is in fact desire and desire alone. Justice is desire and not law.' The crucial point in the trial turns precisely upon Farlan's essentialist claim that 'nothing is stronger than the eternal law of the universe'; to which Reeves retorts: 'This is a court of justice and not of law.' In Goodrich's terms, the film's court might be seen as a fusion of the 'courts of conscience' of spiritual law and of medieval chivalry. Within these 'repressed jurisdictions', the issues at stake in the case are not illogical: Peter appeals for an extension of his earthly life on the basis of having acquired an amorous or chivalrous obligation as a result of heavenly negligence.

Unsurprisingly, the trial barely addresses the theological issue of divine error (is the collection 'service' in some way distinct from God's will and omnipotence?), other than when Reeves insists that Peter's life is not separable from his person; therefore he cannot be said to have 'borrowed' twenty hours. Instead, the hearing deals mainly with how his claimed love for June can be 'proved'; and whether a consequent life in England is a suitable fate for an American woman. The first question poses a paradox: how can either Peter or June 'prove' their love is genuine and will last, without being given time to do so? Poetic 'evidence' of June's love, her tear while watching Peter's operation, has been gathered on a rose ('our only real evidence') and will form the basis of Reeves's opening speech to the reconstituted jury: 'Here in this tear are love and truth and friendship. These qualities and these alone can build a new world today and must build a better world tomorrow.'

But before this, the question of Britain's reputation must be addressed by focusing on the jury – a figure *en abyme* for the cinema audience itself and the film's most direct admission that it is appealing to international public opinion. The shooting script had envisaged a more elaborate introduction of the representative jury. Faced with such a vast audience, the judge would ask if they felt disturbed, and when five said they did, a series of trick shots would show them subjectively seeing only an empty amphitheatre – while the sixth, the Irish 'Sinn Fein rebel', would see a full house, conforming to stereotypical Irish sociability. However, a note in Powell's handwriting questions 'whether we should not cut this gag of seeing the audience … it characterises the Jury too early'. Clearly that view prevailed and we do not see the jury individually until Farlan accuses Reeves of trying to influence its members unfairly and introduces them: a French soldier of the Napoleonic period, a Boer from the Transvaal, a Russian, a Chinese, an Indian and an Irishman. While Farlan enlarges on the theme that any international jury will have reasons to hate Britain and praises America as the home of liberty, Reeves observes mildly that there is little practical difference between the freedoms enjoyed in both countries, before delivering his dramatic counterstroke – 'I choose a jury of Americans' (which provokes the clash over Law and Justice). The new jury, of course, has the same ethnic composition as before – and its first decision is to ask for Peter and June to be heard in person – an intimation of American fairness and informality – which prompts the trial's move to earth, when legal and medical jurisdiction are brought together as the court enters the operating theatre.

This interlude also marks a change of direction in the argument, from the ideology of the national, to the personal, or existential. Farlan's questioning of Peter leads to his challenge: 'Are you willing to die for her?' Peter nearly falls into the trap, before responding that he would rather live. Next, June is awakened from her 'sleep' and similarly challenged, now by Reeves, to 'take Peter's place in the other world'. This trope both rhymes Farlan's challenge – now real, while the other was rhetorical – but also powerfully evokes the classical precedent of Alcestis and Admetus, as noted earlier. Reeves asks the judge to restrain Peter so that the test can be real: June mounts the escalator – at which point Farlan warns, 'Take care, Dr Reeves! In the whole universe nothing is stronger than the law.' The stairway starts to move, carrying June to her fate: then it shudders to a halt, as if unable to resolve the contradiction between necessity and free-will. Reeves responds triumphantly: 'Yes, Mr Farlan, nothing is stronger than the law in the universe, but on earth nothing is stronger than love.'

Following the film's legal trajectory, the issue is that of jurisdiction: does the universe (abstract reason) or earth (humanity) have jurisdiction in this intermediate zone? According to physics, medicine and probability, Peter should be dead – but according to the code of love, flying in the face of reason and convention, Peter's and June's passion can cancel these and win for them a future. In mythic terms, the lovers have emerged from their ordeals, like Tamino and Pamina in *The Magic Flute*. But historically, amid attempts to define individuals according to ideology (the

Second World War victors and vanquished), they represent the triumph of the individual in the face of history – exceptions to the conventions of national stereotyping. The maxim that ends this scene – 'the rights of the uncommon man must always be respected' – has become for some evidence of Powell/Pressburger's Toryism or anti-socialism. But surely there is no implication here that the *common* man's rights should *not* be respected; rather that he who dares may enlarge his and others' rights in the face of 'necessity'. And here we may see a link with the rise of existentialism as an influential post-war philosophy. Sartre's essay, 'Existentialism and Humanism', argued that to choose one's own freedom was unavoidably to choose freedom for others, to treat them as free agents and ends in themselves.[115] In this context, the legal-philosophical moral of *AMOLAD* coincides more closely with the progressive intellectual climate of 1945–6 than it might appear to do – as well as subverting the 'statist' legalism of the epoch by appeal to a fictive jurisdiction which challenges, in Goodrich's term, 'the phantasm of an all-powerful law'.

The Matter of England

AMOLAD has persistently failed to qualify as a 'proper' British film because it is insufficiently 'realist', too whimsical, too equivocal, too pretentious – too much; and yet not enough. The very idea of commonsense realist aesthetics is what it resists, as John Ellis argued:

> The film is centrally concerned with the problems of representation, and with producing a scepticism about notions of realism. ... What [it] does, then, is to question the very notion of the analysis of films in terms of 'content'.[116]

But however sound this semiotic defence, is it enough to claim the point of the film lies in its continued 'dislocation between two discourses'? What of its 'matter' – poised between life and death, war and peace, fantasy and reality – its humour, beauty and mysticism? One context which helps explain some of the film's strange power and poetry has too often been ignored.

English Neo-Romanticism and its adjunct the New Apocalypse have generally been ignored in favour of later, post-war cultural currents, such as The Movement, the Angry Young Men and Pop, leaving the 40s crudely defined in terms of wartime documentary realism followed by post-war melodrama. And yet, as David Mellor notes, Neo-Romanticism was influential across the arts in Britain. It was also, arguably, the moment at which Surrealism and Expressionism took on their distinctive English forms. Inspired by these movements and by D. H. Lawrence's *Apocalypse* (1931), the writers associated with the 'New Apocalypse' – including the poets G. S. Fraser, Norman MacCaig, Vernon Watkins and Dylan Thomas – produced a series of wartime anthologies, culminating in Henry Treece's 1946 manifesto *How I See Apocalypse*. Neo-Romanticism was mainly a movement of visionary painters – Cecil Collins, John Piper, Ceri Richards and Graham Sutherland were among its leading exponents – but many of these were active in other media, as writers, print-makers and stage designers. Several were associated with Dartington Hall, where Heckroth taught; and others would remain Powell's ideal collaborators for the artists' films he proposed in the 50s.[117]

Mellor unhesitatingly includes Powell and Pressburger within its ranks, particularly for their romantic treatment of British landscape in its archetypal and psychological dimensions in *A Canterbury Tale* and *IKWIG!* But the human figure was also present in Neo-Romanticism, in idealised and mythic forms, and Mellor sees the image of Peter Carter, 'resurrected from the sea, yet [failing] to ascend to heaven', in this light. He places him between Keith Vaughan's 1942 *Apocalyptic Figure* – 'a Blakean man ... supernatural, untouched in triumphant clouds and flame' – and 'a revived elemental warrior, like the risen soldier's body David Jones drew as a frontispiece to *In Parenthesis* (1937)'.[118] An older artist associated with this movement in his last years provides another link between the theme of flight and transcendence. Paul Nash, already cited for his views on colour cinema, served as an official War Artist in both world wars; and in the second, he was particularly fascinated by planes viewed as 'personalities' and by 'aerial creatures', compounded from a surreal mixture of cloud, vegetable and floral forms. These 'aerial flowers', as Nash termed them, renewed the inspiration he had taken from Sir Thomas Browne's image of 'the soul visiting the Mansions of the Dead'. Unable to fly himself, he embarked on an intense imaginative exploration of 'that mysterious domain of the air', recognising that this was also a way of thinking about death. *AMOLAD* begins with a solitary flyer facing death and ends with a victory. Peter's last line, 'we won,' signifies not only the success of the operation, and winning its analogue, his 'case', but also the end of the war itself and a return to life.

We might reconstruct *AMOLAD*, then, as beginning amid apocalypse, with the last moments of war and life leading to heavenly judgment. It then reworks the pastoral/Arthurian myth so dear to English art: the return to an Edenic Albion, a paradise garden, a castle in which a fair lady is to be won. This 'parfit, gentil knyght' of the air is beset by the temptations of two former friends, France and America, both urging capitulation to a universal law. But the code of courtly love demands that our hero fights on and, thanks to the sacrifice of *his* champion, he wins against all odds, securing the right to live. To interpret the film's allegory thus is of course to invite scepticism: can it *really* support such a 'poetic' superstructure? I would claim that it does, using humour and a sophisticated version of the modern 'uncanny' (discussed below), to defuse disbelief. Its companion work in British cinema is Humphrey Jennings's *A Diary for Timothy* (also released in 1946), also consciously bestriding the passage from war to an uncertain peace, with an apostrophic commentary written by Forster, addressed to the infant Timothy in the form of a 'prospect of England'. Jennings's film is easier to appreciate, even to take for granted; although, as Lindsay Anderson insisted, it is actually dense with 'associations and implications so multifarious' that they can hardly be grasped in the first viewings.[119] The same, I believe, is true of *AMOLAD*, although it reaches further and deeper than Jennings could in a short film masquerading as 'documentary', carrying forward the themes of Eliot's neo-apocalytic *Four Quartets*, and contemporary with Britten's equally controversial attempts to invent a viable English operatic idiom in *Peter Grimes* (1945) and the neo-classical *Rape of Lucretia* (1946).

A Wartime Uncanny

It is not difficult to imagine why the war should have encouraged a belief, or hope, that death is not final; and that providence or coincidence might be at work to forestall disaster. But *AMOLAD* is not a ghost story, conventional or otherwise; it might be described as a rational (or rationalist) fantasy, in which an hallucination is shown to be 'explained' by medical science. And yet it conveys an 'uncanny' feeling, in Freud's sense, because the very scale and logic of Peter's heavenly fantasy lends conviction to what we know to be merely imagined.[120] The religious or childish view of death as the soul being taken to another place is here no longer expressed in archaic language or classical imagery, but made vivid and modern – in fact literal. This is perhaps the true significance of the colour/monochrome division:

heaven seems more documentary than a gaudy earth, upsetting our normal reality–fantasy schema. Peter 'should' be dead, but he exists as a double of himself in the limbo of the stairway or out of time in the operating theatre. Here, *AMOLAD* ingeniously updates the traditional notion of the *doppelgänger*, which had been analysed by Otto Rank in 1914, taking account of the recent first film version of *The Student of Prague*. Freud in turn drew on Rank's analysis in his account of the uncanny, agreeing that the double 'was originally an insurance against the destruction of the ego, "an energetic denial of the power of death"'. Peter is that 'energetic denial' incarnate, as he insists on arguing his case; yet the effect is, to repeat, *not* ghostly, but rather rational. Reality and fantasy are not so much blurred, as in the 'classic' (i.e. romantic) uncanny, but evenly matched and causally correlated. *AMOLAD* might stand as a rare example of the 'intellectual uncanny', with its poetry counterpointed by medicine – recalling, of course, that earlier example of the Neo-Platonic physician, Sir Thomas Browne, as Powell and Pressburger clearly intended. But unlike Browne it is strikingly, and surprisingly, devoid of conventional religious sentiment.

In this respect, it bears comparison with the two other great wartime supernatural films, *Les Visiteurs du soir* (1942) and *A Guy Named Joe* (1944). Carné's and Prévert's film is an allegory, set in 1485, in which the devil sows confusion within a castle by sending two seducers, before he is himself outwitted by the heroine's willingness to sacrifice herself for one of the emissaries. The devil apparently was intended to be read as Hitler

The allegorical lovers preserved as statues to thwart the devil in Carné's *Les Visiteurs du soir*

and Anne as France, still able to resist morally under occupation; but within this schematic political allegory, there is a more compelling fable about, again, free-will and determination. Even the supernatural characters are shown to be conformist, like all the mortals apart from the spirited figure of Anne, who pursues her love beyond the risk of damnation, as June risks death on Peter's behalf.

By comparison, Victor Fleming's *A Guy Named Joe* seems at first merely sentimental: a dead pilot is sent back to earth to act as guardian angel for a younger comrade who becomes his girl's new suitor. The focus, however, is not on this new romance, but on the dead flyer's struggle to master his jealousy and become a true guardian – a role that is explained to him by the celestial C.O. (Lionel Barrymore) in a scene of memorable restraint and eloquence. Unexpectedly, perhaps, one of the film's most enthusiastic supporters was Eisenstein, who wrote passionately about its moral message, that 'there is an unbreakable chain of human experience ... a creative heritage which is transmitted down the generations'.[121] Here we see another facet of the wartime uncanny: use of the supernatural to create a symbolic melodrama about human interdependence and the moral lessons to be learned under war conditions.

Compared with his unstinted praise for *A Guy Named Joe*, Eisenstein was dismissive of *AMOLAD* in a reference to the closing eyelid near the end of his essay on 'stereoscopic cinema'. This effect, along with Robert Montgomery's ultra-subjective *Lady in the Lake*, are 'examples of the pathological introspection to which western "creators" are turning, having broken with healthy realism to serve reaction'.[122] The tone of the last phrase indicates that this part of the article must have been written after the political directive to attack the Anglo-American alliance. But even if it is hardly 'fair' to *AMOLAD*, it usefully links the film with a widespread tendency towards subjectivism in the mid-40s – a 'sign of the times', as Eisenstein describes the pistol turned towards the camera in another arch-exhibit, Hitchcock's *Spellbound*.

Spellbound might be grouped with *It's a Wonderful Life* and *AMOLAD* to form a therapeutic trio of 1946, all making ostentatious use of subjective and reflexive tropes. In the first, the patient is 'cured' of his murderous compulsion by interpretation of his symbolic dreams; and in the second, an angel reveals the hidden virtue of George's apparently unsuccessful life by conjuring a vision of what his early death would have meant. All three films show their heroes 'saved' by an elaborate metaphysical machinery which indeed aims to intensify the spectator's identification; and yet *AMOLAD* is the only one to go explicitly beyond the personal to embrace notions of the national and the international. In this sense, however unacceptable its politics were for Stalinist Russia in 1947, it can hardly be tarred with the naïve or decadent subjectivism identified by Eisenstein. On the contrary, what it proposes is a *negotiation* between the realms of the material and the ideological, recognising the powers of each, and offering the spectator a more 'objective' position – a seat amid the heavenly tribunal, able to weigh up the historical and dramatic 'evidence'.

In this respect, the chess plot may also be of more significance than at first appears. The Conductor tries to tempt Peter by offering him the opportunity to pit his skill against the great chess masters; and he 'borrows' Alekhine's famous book of his best games, only to return it in an extraordinary transitional shot which introduces the final sequence of Peter waking up in hospital. As a token of Peter's life, the book tumbles from one photographic world to another within the same shot. The figure of the chess player, who has pitted his will and intellect against the power of death, consolidates an image of rational post-war man. Even though the real Alekhine had died earlier in that same year, chess remains supra-individual – while providing a metaphor of human struggle that Bergman would make central to his neo-apocalyptic *The Seventh Seal* a decade later.

Alekhine's book joins the two worlds to conclude *AMOLAD*

EPILOGUE

. . . .

AFTERLIFE

Jonathan Miller wrote evocatively in 1992 about having first seen *AMOLAD* as a child in 1947, when he was seized with 'the idea that there was some vast, dazzling eternity out there, and in the surface of ordinary reality one might find some narrow slit through which one could catch a glimpse of it'.[123] As an adult 'radical materialist', however, knowing that 'there's no door in the wall … it just seems a wonderfully English piece of camp'. Miller can perhaps stand for a continuing English tradition of hostility to the English fantastic. Indeed, for his 1996 production of *A Midsummer Night's Dream*, he expressly rejected the 'exorbitant demand for enchantment' and erased 'the difference between the natural and supernatural characters of the play'.[124] But *AMOLAD* finds itself in tune with many contemporary time-travel narratives (*Bill and Ted's Bogus Journey* duly pays homage); and with the 'new supernaturalism' of films ranging from Spielberg's remake of *A Guy Named Joe* as *Always*, followed by *Ghost*, *Truly, Madly, Deeply* and *City of Angels* (itself a remake of Wenders's *Wings of Desire*, but also evoking the *doppelgänger* effect of *AMOLAD*, when souls depart their bodies), up to *A Life Less Ordinary* (produced in 1997 by Pressburger's grandson, Andrew Macdonald) in which the heavenly enforcers become earthly gangsters.

AMOLAD never disappeared from view, in the way that *Blimp* and *A Canterbury Tale* did after being re-edited. But it was difficult to see during the 60s and 70s; and even more difficult in the 80s, when the remake rights were sold by The Archers and Rank to Columbia, although nothing ever came of this. In 1994, it was adapted as a stage musical (more successfully than *The Red Shoes*) under the title *Stairway to Heaven*, winning an award for its novice creators.[125]

In 1997 the music of *AMOLAD* was heard again at the end of *Robinson in Space*, Patrick Keiller's disenchanted survey of 'this island now'. The last words of the film's narration refer to its mysterious Crusoe-esque hero, Robinson, finding his utopia; followed by a silhouetted image of bridges across a river accompanied by the stairway motif, in what might suggest an oblique intimation of crossing to 'the other side'. In the context of Keiller's passionate engagement with England's cultural landscape, the effect is to remobilise *AMOLAD*, as if summoning it to bear witness for a nation once again unsure of its identity and future.

Materially, the film has also been restored on both sides of the Atlantic, making both its rich Technicolor tones more tactile and its pearly monochrome more luminous. And, following its video cassette release, there is now a DVD edition, with a supplement featuring Jack Cardiff digitally placed on the same escalator that he photographed over fifty years earlier. The electronic revolution has brought *AMOLAD* within everyone's grasp, able to be run forwards and backwards, frozen at will. Whatever aura may have been lost in the process, it has now acquitted the ubiquity and familiarity of a classic, capable of being venerated and also of attracting such parodies as the sketch from BBC 2's *Big Train* in which a circus of 'doomed pilots' compete for the attention of a bored radio controller.

Openness to multiple readings and a 'surplus of signifier' are intrinsic features of the modern classic work, according to Kermode.[126] It is time to ask if *AMOLAD* satisfies these and other criteria, to be considered a truly major work, requiring no alibis. The passage of time, I want to suggest, enables us to historicise the 40s and so see the political intervention of *AMOLAD* more clearly. Its royal premiere, at first sight merely contingent, underlines the parallel with Renaissance masques, 'Spectacles of State' in Jonson's phrase. Equally, our distance in time allows a better appreciation of its sheer range of cultural references and audio-visual poetic tropes – wit rather than whimsy. John Ellis's important claim that the film disturbs simplistic notions of cinematic realism is true, but it does not deal with what is also created, which is a distinctive poetry of heightened cinematic effect.[127] Though Frances Yates' revelatory writings on hermeticism in the English Renaissance, it has become clear that theatre itself then served as a moral emblem. In *AMOLAD*, cinema is vested with something of the same significance, becoming a modern allegory of freewill versus determinism and of a post-Einsteinian concept of space becoming relative and 'local'.[128]

Most important of all, the spectacle of *AMOLAD* turns out to be intrinsic to its themes. The modernized Jacob's Ladder of the stairway is not a symbol of transcendence, but a trap in this anti-utopian and quite secular allegory. Despite Scott's 'love is heaven and heaven is love', love is shown as temporal, human and only to be enjoyed on earth. After its spectacular display of cinematic magic, and intricate metaphysics of identity and mortality, *AMOLAD* finally articulates the post-war yearning for 'normal' lives and deaths. This modernist masque deploys its dazzling version of Inigo Jones' 'pictures with Light and Motion', not to amaze but to achieve what Johnson insisted masques were or should be: 'the mirrors of man's life'.[129]

NOTES

· ·

1 Ian Christie, 'Out of this World', *Times Higher Education Supplement*, 5 July 1996.
2 Two poems by John Pudney, 'Missing' and 'Johnny-in-the-Clouds', are attributed to 'Flight Lt. David Archdale' (Michael Redgrave), one of the pilots killed in *The Way to the Stars*. The latter, spoken by Redgrave, provides the film's epilogue – and makes *AMOLAD*, with its poet-pilot, a kind of sequel. *The Way to the Stars* was greatly admired for its emotional restraint on release in mid-1945. For a well-documented account of the film, see Anthony Aldgate and Jeffrey Richards, *Britain Can Take It: The British Cinema in the Second World War* (Oxford: Basil Blackwell, 1986), pp. 277–98.
3 *The Ghost Goes West* (René Clair, 1936) featured a Scottish ghost following his castle to America; *Here Comes Mr Jordan* (Alexander Hall, 1941), much imitated, had a boxer accidentally classified dead being helped by his guardian angel to find a substitute body; and *Heaven Can Wait* (Ernst Lubitsch, 1943), the only one of these in colour, was set in Hell, as a deceased roué recalls his mortal adventures. All three were mentioned in 1946 by various reviewers in relation to *AMOLAD*.
4 Humphrey Swingler, *Our Time*, December 1946, p. 112. A 'yes, but …' pattern of criticism was first identified by John Ellis, 'Watching Death at Work: An Analysis of *A Matter of Life and Death*', in Ian Christie (ed.), *Powell, Pressburger and Others* (London: British Film Institute, 1978), p. 86.
5 Jonathan Bate traces Shakespeare's evolving reputation with great subtlety; and contextu-alises Ben Jonson's famous criticisms (implausibility, lack of 'Art' and 'little Latin') within a general admiration, in *The Genius of Shakespeare* (London: Picador, 1997), pp. 26–32. The hallmark of a classic, according to Kermode, is its ability to support multiple interpretations – having a 'surplus of signifier' – across time, becoming 'timeless' through a process of allegory. Frank Kermode, *The Classic: Literary Images of Permanence and Change* (Cambridge, MA: Harvard University Press, 1983). I have learned much from these stimulating books about the processes of reputation and influence.

6 The fullest of these accounts, embellished with much culinary detail, is in Michael Powell, *A Life in Movies* (London: Heinemann, 1986), pp. 455–7. This places the meeting during the post-production of *A Canterbury Tale*, probably March–April 1944.
7 Presumably the Ministry of Information had suggested the Anglo-American co-operation theme of the two flying films written by Rattigan, *Journey Together* (Boulting, 1944) and *The Way to the Stars* (1945), as well as officially sponsoring the dramatised guide for American arrivals, *A Welcome to Britain* (Asquith, 1943).
8 Powell, *A Life in Movies*, pp. 456–8.
9 W. B. Yeats, 'An Irish Airman Forsees His Death' (1919); Bertolt Brecht, *Der Lindberghflug* [The Lindberg Flight], a radio oratorio with music by Kurt Weill and Paul Hindemith (1929); W. H. Auden, 'Consider' (c.1930) and, with Christopher Isherwood, *The Dog Beneath the Skin* (1935); Antoine de Saint-Exupéry, *Vol de nuit* [Night Flight] (1932).
10 On flyers as defective heroes, see Peter Wollen, '*La Régle du jeu* and Modernity', *Film Studies* no. 1, 1999, pp. 5–13.
11 'An Airman to his Mother', reprinted as a leaflet from *The Times*, 4 June 1940, with the subtitle 'My Earthly Mission is Fulfilled'. Wilfred Owen used Horace's phrase, 'It is sweet and becoming to die for one's country', as the ironic title of one of his bitter elegies.
12 Richard Hillary, *The Last Enemy* (1942), p. 28.
13 Arthur Koestler, 'The Birth of a Myth', *Horizon*, April 1943; reprinted as 'In Memory of Richard Hillary', in *The Yogi and the Commissar and Other Essays* (London: Jonathan Cape, 1945), pp. 46–67.
14 Pressburger's unfilmed script, *A Face Like England* (1957), featured a flyer whose damaged face becomes emblematic of the nation; while Powell included the story of an Italian anti-fascist poet-pilot in his television series treatment *Thirteen Ways to Kill a Poet* (1970).
15 Kevin Macdonald, *Emeric Pressburger: The Life and Death of a Screenwriter* (London: Faber and Faber, 1994), p. 25.
16 Powell, *A Life in Movies*, p. 502.
17 Ibid., p. 514.

18 Samuel Johnson was responsible in 1773 for labelling Donne and his followers 'metaphysical' because of their use of ingenious conceits.
19 Alexander Pope (1688–1744) had his first major success with *The Rape of the Lock* in 1712–14, a satirical mock-heroic epic.
20 David Mellor, 'Sketch for an Historical Portrait of Humphrey Jennings', in Mary-Lou Jennings (ed.), *Humphrey Jennings: Film-Maker, Painter, Poet* (London: British Film Institute, 1982), p. 70.
21 Quoted in Stephen Orgel, *The Jonsonian Masque* (Cambridge, MA: Harvard, 1965), p. 3. A fuller account of this argument appears in my 'Gegen den Naturalismus: Raum und Zeit in Filmen von Michael Powell und Emeric Pressburger' [Against Naturalism: Space and Time in the Films of Powell and Pressburger], in Andreas Rost (ed.), *Zeit, Schnitt, Raum* (Frankfurt: Verlag der Autoren, 1997), pp. 95–119.
22 Robert Arden, recruited to play one of the GIs, quoted in James Howard, *Michael Powell* (London: Batsford, 1996), pp. 54–5.
23 Played by Robert Atkins, a noted Shakespearean producer at the time.
24 References for Barrie's lost film, *The Real Thing At Last*, are given in Luke McKernan and Olwen Terris (eds), *Walking Shadows: Shakespeare in the National Film and Television Archive* (London: British Film Institute, 1994), pp. 6, 23n.
25 Stanley Wells discusses this debate in his introduction to *A Midsummer Night's Dream* (London: Penguin, 1995), pp. 12–14.
26 Alexander Pope built a camera obscura in his garden at Twickenham around 1744, but they were most popular in Britain during the nineteenth century. For detailed references, see Hermann Hecht, *Pre-Cinema History* (London: Bowker-Sauer/British Film Institute, 1993), pp. 431–2; 451–2.
27 'Prospero studying his mirrors. Since Galileo his mind has leapt onward towards parabolic mirrors, periscopes, and television.' Michael Powell, 'The Tempest: Technical Shooting Script', typescript, n.d., p. 11. See also Judith Buchanan, "Like ths insubstantial pageant faded": Michael Powell's *The Tempest*', *Film Studies* no. 2, 2000 pp. 79–90.

28 Apollo has 'tricked the Fates' so that Admetis can escape death if someone else will take his place. Euripides, *Alcestis and Other Plays*, ed. and trans. Philip Vellacott (Harmondsworth: Penguin, 1953), pp. 121–2.
29 On influences on Auden, see Michael Sidnell, *Dances of Death: the Group Theatre of London in the Thirties* (London: Faber, 1984), Ch. 3 *et seq*.
30 Peter Ackroyd, *T. S. Eliot: A Life* (New York: Simon and Schuster, 1984), pp. 227–8.
31 See Gillian Beer's illuminating introduction to Virginia Woolf, *Between the Acts* (Harmondsworth: Penguin, 1992), pp. xxxii–xxxiv.
32 See Ian Christie (ed.), *The Life and Death of Colonel Blimp* (London: Faber, 1994), pp. 173–5.
33 There seems to be no commonly accepted term for this trope in English, other than the 'hypodiegetic narrative' proposed by Shlomith Rimmon-Kenan, *Narrative Fiction: Contemporary Poetics* (London: Methuen, 1983), pp. 92–3. On *mis en abyme*, see Jean Ricardou, *Le nouveau roman* (Paris: Seuil, 1978), pp. 47–50.
34 Frigyes Karinthy, *A Journey Round My Skull* (London: Faber, 1938). This is described at 'the most durable prose work' by Karinthy (1888–1938), otherwise known for his interest in the fantastic, the grotesque and scientific utopias, in T. Klaniczay, J. Szauder and M. Szabolcsi, *History of Hungarian Literature* (Budapest: Corvina Press/Collet's Holdings, 1964), p. 215.
35 Karinthy, *A Journey Round My Skull*, p. 13.
36 Ibid., p. 241.
37 Ibid., pp. 244–5.
38 Kevin Gough-Yates, 'Interview with Michael Powell', in *Michael Powell in Collaboration with Emeric Pressburger* (London: British Film Institute, 1971), p. 10.
39 Powell, *A Life in Movies*, p. 458.
40 Diane Broadbent Friedman, 'A Matter of Fried Onions', *Seizure* no. 1, 1992, pp. 307–10. See also David Badder, 'Powell and Pressburger: The War Years', *Sight and Sound*, Spring 1979, pp. 8–12.

41 'Significance of Auditory and Visual Hallucinations', British Medical Association Scientific Meetings, 26–8 July, *The Lancet*, 19 August 1939, pp. 426–7.

42 *Dann Schon Lieber Lebertran*, Ufa, 1930. Based on a story by Kästner, summarised in Christie (ed.), *Powell, Pressburger and Others*, p. 7.

43 The Sand-Man appears in Hoffmann's *Nachtstücken*. In Offenbach's opera, on which the film is based, he becomes the recurrent character of Lindorf-Coppelius-Dapertutto (the collector of souls in the Venetian episode) – Dr Miracle, all played by Robert Helpmann. Freud discussed 'The Sand-Man' at length in his essay, 'The Uncanny' (1919), in Albert Dickson (ed.), *Art and Literature*, The Penguin Freud Library, Vol. 14 (Harmondsworth: Penguin Books, 1985), pp. 347–60.

44 'On the Gate: a Tale of '16', was begun in 1916, but according to Rider Haggard, Kipling's wife would not let him publish it for fear of giving offence, until it appeared in 1926 and was collected in *Debits and Credits* in that year. Quotations from the Penguin edition, edited by Sandra Kemp (London: 1987), pp. 235–52.

45 In Greek mythology, Hermes was supposedly the son of the sky (Zeus) and the plains (Maia), and as god of the wind, served as messenger and gatherer of souls of the dead. Together with his Roman equivalent, Mercury, he is the source for the Robin Goodfellow-Puck-Ariel figure invoked by Shakespeare and Kipling.

46 *Religio medici* (1642) means 'The Religion of a Doctor'. The quotation is from Part II, Section 9. L. C. Martin (ed.), *Religio Medici and Other Works* (Oxford: Clarendon Press, 1964), p. 67.

47 Ibid., Part I, Section 9, p. 9. *Hydriotaphia, or Urn Burial* (1658) rises to even greater heights of eloquence.

48 The attribution of 'His Pilgrimage', also known as 'The Passionate Man's Pilgrimage' to Sir Walter Raleigh (1554–1618) is now thought uncertain.

49 Macdonald, *Pressburger*, p. 234.

50 I am grateful to Andrew Youdell for this information.

51 See, for instance, the miniature pocket edition published by Samuel Bagster and Sons (n.d.), with an introduction by Robert Louis Stevenson praising the simple anonymous illustrations by 'a Bunyan of the pencil … literal to the verge of folly' (p. viii). The Jacob's Ladder episode is on pp. 314–15 in this edition.

52 Plate 9, The Gates of Paradise (1793), in William Blake, *Poems and Prophecies* (New York: Alfred Knopf, The Everyman's Library, 1991), p. 301. See also his Genesis illustration.

53 The film was adapted from Selma Lagerlöf's epic novel sequence *Jerusalem* (1901–2), which led to her winning the Nobel prize for literature in 1907. Sjöstrom's *Ingmarssönerna* was the first of four films based on the novels, which tell of an evangelist persuading pious rural Swedes to follow him in a disastrous pilgrimage to the Holy Land.

54 'Auguries of Innocence', in Blake, *Poems and Prophecies*, p. 333. Blake was strongly influenced by Swedenborgian mysticism and by Neo-Platonism.

55 On the rose as an alchemical and mystical symbol, see Frances A. Yates, *The Rosicrucian Enlightenment* (London: Routledge, 1972), pp. 64–5.

56 Myers's book was published posthumously in 1903, after his death in 1901; then in an abridged edition in 1919, which was reissued by the Pelegrin Trust/Pilgrim Books, Norwich, in 1992. Paul Hammond pointed out allusions in a private communication.

57 These quotations from Myers's posthumous *Fragments of Prose and Poetry* are quoted in a Biographical Sketch preceding the Pilgrim Books edition, p. 63.

58 For instance: 'In my Father's house are many mansions. … I go to prepare a place for you,' John 14.2.

59 J. W. Dunne (1875–1949) also published, with increasing ambition, *The Serial Universe* (1934) and *Nothing Dies* (1940).

60 Priestley characterised Dunne as 'as far removed from any suggestion of the seer, the sage, the crank and crackpot, as it is possible to imagine', in *Man and Time* (London: Aldus Books, 1964; republished by Bloomsbury

Books, 1989), p. 244. Behind Dunne and Priestley, however, stood Ouspensky and his guru Gurdjieff, guardians of 'the Work', and Jung.

61 *Thunder Rock* (1942), based on an anti-isolationist play by Robert Ardrey, starred Michael Redgrave, and was greeted with wide admiration. *The Halfway House* (1943), directed by Basil Dearden for Ealing, fared less well critically; although many of the same personnel worked on the acclaimed compendium *Dead of Night*, a year later, which uses a recurrent dream structure.

62 H. H. Wollenberg, 'Statistics', *The Penguin Film Review* no. 4, 1947, p. 118. Although this would rise by 1947 to thirty-five million per week, or four-fifths of the total population, since more than half of the over-35 population rarely attended, the 40s 'myth of the universal audience' should be treated with caution, according to David Docherty, David Morrison and Michael Tracey, *The Last Picture Show? Britain's Changing Film Audience* (London: British Film Institute, 1987), pp. 16–17.

63 'I am in films because of the Holy Spirit,' Rank famously declared, as quoted in Alan Wood, *Mr Rank* (London: Hodder and Stoughton, 1952), p. 67. Max Weber traced a close connection between nonconformism and the rise of capitalism in *The Protestant Ethic and the Spirit of Capitalism* (1904).

64 Macdonald, *Pressburger*, p. 197. This contradicts the chronology in *A Life in Movies*, where Powell claimed that the invitation came after '… *one of our aircraft is missing*'s trade show, in March (p. 397).

65 *Kinematograph Weekly*, 6 September 1942.

66 Powell, *A Life in Movies*, p. 459.

67 The Michael Powell papers include a confidential memorandum from Powell to Rank, 'A New Design for Films', dated February 1945; a listing of essential equipment needed for 'process film production' (as the project was then known), dated 1 February 1945; and the full report by Rawnsley, dated 4 August 1945. This approach became known as 'independent frame' because it proposed that the mechanical and electronic 'framework' should be independent from the actors' playing.

68 Macdonald records that Pressburger signed a round-robin letter of protest against the scheme and that it threatened to split The Archers, *Pressburger*, p. 263.

69 Rawnsley later explained his scheme in a 'detailed review', in *The Cine-Technician*, March–April 1948, pp. 50–6, coinciding with the release of the first official IF film, *Warning to Wantons* (Donald Wilson, 1948), followed by an Eric Linklater adaptation, *Poet's Pub* (Wilson) and Noël Coward's *The Astonished Heart* (Fisher, 1949).

70 Powell called it his 'last uncomposed film' in a speech, 'The Influence of Music on Colour Cinematography', referring to his experiments with shooting to pre-recorded music from *Black Narcissus* onwards. Powell papers (n.d., but probably *c.*1961).

71 Powell, *A Life in Movies*, p. 49.

72 On the history of Technicolor and its British branch, see Duncan Petrie, *The British Cinematographer* (London: British Film Institute, 1996), pp. 39ff.

73 Gorham A. Kindem, 'Hollywood's Conversion to Colour: The Technological, Economic and Aesthetic Factors', *Journal of the University Film Association* vol. XXXI no. 2, Spring 1979.

74 Jack Cardiff, *Magic Hour: The Life of a Cameraman* (London: Faber, 1996), pp. 41ff.

75 Paul Nash, 'The Colour Film', in Charles Davy (ed.), *Footnotes to the Film* (London: Lovat Dickinson, 1938), p. 125.

76 Nash quoted Natalie Kalmus 'without comment except italics' on *Wings of the Morning*: 'In this picture *we are trying to preserve one level of colour throughout*' (p. 126).

77 Cardiff, *Magic Hour*, p. 77.

78 Ibid., p. 86.

79 Powell, *A Life in Movies*, p. 498.

80 Details from a caption in the 'book of the film', Eric Warman, *A Matter of Life and Death* (London: World Film Publications, 1946).

81 Giambattista Piranesi's various etchings on the fantastic dungeon theme, especially the *Invenzioni capricosi di carceri* of 1745 and 1761–5, have been highly influential in the twentieth century. On the modernist design sources and history of Korda's production, see

Christopher Frayling, *Things to Come* (London: British Film Institute, 1995), especially pp. 62ff.
82 Powell, *A Life in Movies*, p. 628.
83 Brunius writing as 'Jacques Borel' in *L'Ecran français* no. 72, November 1946; Bazin, *L'Ecran français* no. 116, September 1946. Both quoted in Roland Lacourbe (ed.), *Question de Vie ou de Mort, L'avant-scène du cinéma* no. 258, December 1980, pp. 45–6.
84 Were other designers actively considered? Junge's letter of 3 April 1946 noted that 'letters have appeared with several names on them except mine.' Held by the Cinemathèque française; and quoted in Charles Affron and Mirella Jona Affron, *Sets in Motion: Art Direction and Film Narrative* (New Jersey: Rutgers University Press, 1995), p. 11.
85 For details and photographs, see Suzanne K. Walther, 'The Dance of Death: Description and Analysis of *The Green Table*', *Choreography and Dance* vol. 2 part 2, 1993, pp. 53–77.
86 Powell, *A Life in Movies*, p. 532.
87 Olivier Assayas reported Powell claiming that Day had 'worked in his early youth with Méliès', but I have been unable to verify this: 'Redécouvrir Michael Powell: l'esprit du temps', *Cahiers du cinéma* no. 321, 1981, p. 11.
88 Powell, *A Life in Movies*, p. 490.
89 David Niven, *The Moon's a Balloon* (London: Coronet Books, 1973), p. 246.
90 Publicity photographs appear in Warman's tie-in book; Powell's account in *A Life in Movies*, pp. 541–4.
91 Cardiff, *Magic Hour*, p. 85.
92 According to the film's original press-kit, confirmed by Kathleen Byron, the five stars' other commitments prevented them from all meeting until the film's launch. The same press material also mentioned that Goring would get his chance to play a non-character part in The Archers' new film, *The Red Shoes*.
93 In a self-portrait questionnaire reproduced in Macdonald, *Pressburger*, p. 204.
94 John Huntley, 'Film Music', *Penguin Film Review* no. 4, p. 19.
95 Paul Nash, 'Aerial Flowers' (1944), in a supplement to the catalogue of the exhibition *Paul Nash: Aerial Creatures*, Imperial War Museum, 1996, p. 13.

96 *Today's Cinema* [including *The Cinema*], 4 September 1946, p. 3.
97 An American industry leader, the President of Universal-International, was quoted as saying, 'British films must secure fair American distribution if restrictions are not to be placed on Hollywood's films in Britain.' He went on to note that the loss of revenue from Britain would materially affect Hollywood production values. *Today's Cinema*, 5 November 1946, p. 1.
98 For instance, in a fashion illustrator's annotated sketch in the *Daily Express*, 1 November 1946. More realistically, under continuing rationing, the press-kit for local newspapers featured Kim Hunter in pyjamas 'which are a good choice at the present time, when we are having to use the minimum of material'.
99 This entrenched cultural suspicion surfaced most explosively in the scandal of Oscar Wilde's trial in 1895, in which 'decadence' was as much at issue as homosexuality; and in the furore around the London Post-Impressionist exhibitions of 1910–12.
100 Christie, *Powell, Pressburger and Others*, p. 87.
101 Gavin Lambert, 'British Films 1947: Survey and Prospects', *Sequence* no. 2, Winter 1947, pp. 9–14. In another article in the same issue, by Lindsay Anderson, Powell and Pressburger are included with Welles and Sam Wood, etc. as film-makers before whom 'we must spend many a tortured hour … squirming, yawning and cursing' (p. 8).
102 Reprinted in Christie, *Powell, Pressburger and Others*, p. 66. Durgnat went on to explore with equal lucidity the political allegory of *AMOLAD* in *A Mirror for England* (London: Faber, 1970), pp. 29–31.
103 The first Powell retrospective took place at the National Film Theatre, London, in 1971, followed by a larger one at the Brussels Filmmuseum in 1973, both organised by Kevin Gough-Yates and accompanied by booklets containing interviews with Powell, and in the former with Pressburger. The author organised a complete retrospective of all extant films directed by Powell and Pressburger which was held at the National Film Theatre in 1978,

accompanied by Christie, *Powell, Pressburger
and Others*, and this was followed by
retrospectives in Locarno, New York, Munich
and Paris during the early 80s.

104 This is the main thrust of my *Arrows of
Desire*, first published in 1985, then expanded
for a second edition (London: Faber, 1994). The
first volume of Powell's memoirs, *A Life in
Movies*, followed in 1986, consolidating the
mythic, romantic account of his life and career
up to 1948.

105 Thomas Elsaesser, '*The Tales of
Hoffmann*', first published in the *Brighton Film
Review*, 1968; reprinted in Christie, *Powell,
Pressburger and Others*, pp. 62–5.

106 Marcia Landy, *British Genres: Cinema and
Society, 1930–1960* (Princeton, NJ: Princeton
University Press, 1991), pp. 154–6.

107 E. W. and M. M. Robson, *The World is My
Cinema* (London: The Sidneyan Society, 1947),
p. 65. Chief among the Society's 'aims', as set
out in the earlier pamphlet, is to insist that 'film
and television must be measured by the critical
test applied by Sir Philip Sidney in 1581 which
has been valid since the classic days of Greek
and Roman civilisation … "*To make to imitate,
and imitate both to delight and teach, and teach to
move men to take that goodness in hand which,
without delight, they would fly as from a
stranger.*"' (p. 31).

108 Recent books continue to feature the
Robsons' extremist views. Scott Salwolke
suggests that 'it is hard to believe Robson [*sic*]
was alone in his views' about *Blimp*, in *The
Films of Michael Powell and the Archers*
(Lanham, MD: Scarecrow Press, 1997), p. 94.
On the contrary, it would be hard to believe that
anyone else believed such paranoid rubbish – or
indeed that the 'Sidneyan Society' had more
than two members.

109 The article originally appeared in *Kultura
iɀhiɀn* [Culture and Life] no. 15, 1947, signed 'B.
S.' and was a riposte to 'a lengthy article' about
the film which had appeared in *British Ally*.
Tom Ruben has drawn my attention to his
quotation from it in a BICC Film Society
programme note in 1967; and it is reproduced in
full as an Appendix in Sue Harper and Vincent
Porter, '*A Matter of Life and Death* – the View

from Moscow', *Historical Journal of Film,
Radio and Television* vol. 9 no. 2, 1989,
pp. 181–8. Harper and Porter were unable to
trace the relevant issue of *British Ally*, but this
could be the article published by the Service
d'Information of the British Embassy in Paris
and quoted in *L'avant-scène du cinéma* no. 258.
Here Roger Manvell suggests that this is 'a
remarkable film which should not be examined
too rigorously in terms of its story treatment,
but that it is a most interesting display of
imaginative technique'. He goes on to criticise
it for inconsistency and exploiting rather than
studying its theme and characters – all charges
which, in effect, 'B. S.' rebuts.

110 Henry Butterfield Ryan, *The Vision of
Anglo-America: the US–UK Alliance and the
Emerging Cold War, 1943–1946* (Cambridge:
Cambridge University Press, 1987), p. 171.

111 FO 371-44574, paper AN 2438, 20 July 1945;
the record of a conversation with B. E. F. Gage,
who had attended the San Francisco Conference
preparing the United Nations Organisation on
behalf of the Foreign Office and remained in the
US to 'take soundings': quoted in Ryan, *The
Vision of Anglo-America*, p. 28.

112 Memorandum prepared by the British
Embassy in Washington on 20 November 1945
as 'confidential guidance … which British
officials in the US might find useful': from the
Atlee papers, Oxford, box 6, file O–P, quoted in
Ryan, *The Vision of Anglo-America*, p. 29.

113 Eisenstein's article, published in the
autumn issue of 1947, also appeared in *Kultura
iɀhiɀn*.

114 Peter Goodrich, *Law in the Courts of
Love: Literature and other Minor Jurisprudences*
(London: Routledge, 1996), p. 3.

115 'I cannot make liberty my aim unless I
make that of others equally my aim' (p. 52).
Peter's dilemma can also be refigured in terms
of existentialism's famous dictum that man's
'existence precedes his essence', since he argues
from the *fact* of his survival to his *right* to live.
Jean-Paul Sartre's lecture, 'L'existentialisme est
un humanisme', given in 1945, was first
published in 1946 and translated into English in
1948 (reference to the Eyre Methuen 1973
edition).

116 Christie, *Powell, Pressburger and Others*, p. 103.

117 Dylan Thomas and Graham Sutherland were among those he planned to involve in a series for television; further details in Christie, *Arrows of Desire* (2nd edn.), p. 107.

118 David Mellor, 'The Body and the Land: Neo-Romantic Art and Culture', in D. Mellor and A. Crozier (eds), *A Paradise Lost: the Romantic Imagination in Britain 1935–1955* (London: Lund Humphries, 1987), p. 26.

119 Lindsay Anderson, 'Only Connect: Some Aspects of the Work of Humphrey Jennings', first published in 1954; reprinted in Jennings, *Humphrey Jennings*, p. 57.

120 Sigmund Freud, 'The Uncanny' (1919); *Standard Edition*, Vol. 17; quotations here from Albert Dickson (ed.), *Art and Literature*, The Penguin Freud Library, Vol. 14 (Harmondsworth: Penguin, 1985), pp. 339–76.

121 S. M. Eisenstein, *Memoires 2*, in Jacques Aumont *et al.* (eds/trans.), *Oeuvres*, Vol. 5 (Paris: Christian Bourgois, 1980), p. 228. Written probably in 1945–6, certainly before 'Purveyors of Spiritual Poison'.

122 Sergei Eisenstein, 'Du cinéma en relief', in François Albera and Naoum Kleiman (eds), *Eisenstein: le mouvement de l'art* (Paris: Editions du Cerf, 1986), p. 152 (my translation). This text was apparently written between 1946 and 1948.

123 *Sunday Telegraph*, 22 March 1992.

124 Quotations from *A Midsummer Night's Dream*, V.1. Miller's 1996 Almeida Theatre production, with designs by the Brothers Quay, was notable for eliminating any difference between the natural and supernatural characters. He remarked in the newspaper review of *AMOLAD*: 'In the theatre I can occasionally get back to the feeling I had about this film and the alternative domain.'

125 *Stairway to Heaven*, by Morgan and Metchear, won the Vivien Ellis prize for new musicals in 1994 and had its premiere at the King's Head Theatre, London.

126 Kermode, *The Classic*, pp. 139-40.

127 Ellis has since hinted at this in a later article on Powell and Pressburger: 'emotion in their films... comes... from being caught up in the spectacle that you are watching'. 'At the Edge of our World', *Vertigo*, Spring 1994, p. 23.

128 Frances Yates, *The Art of Memory* (London: Routledge, 1966) and *The Theatre of the World* (London: Routledge, 1969).

129 Ben Jonson, *Works*, ed. C. H. Herford and P. and E. Simpson, (Oxford: Oxford University Press, 1925-52), vol. VIII, p. 735.

Publisher's note: the print of *A Matter of Life and Death* in the National Film and Television Archive was fully restored by the Archive from original nitrate three-strip camera negatives acquired from Rank Film Distributors.

CREDITS
. . . .
A Matter of Life and Death

GB
1946
GB trade show
12 November 1946
GB release
30 November 1946
General Film Distributors
(Rank)
US release
March 1947
as *Stairway to Heaven*
Universal
Production company
The Archers
**Written, produced and
directed by**
Michael Powell and Emeric
Pressburger
Assistant producer
George R. Busby
Unit manager
Robert C. Foord
Assistant directors
Parry Jones Jr, Paul Kelly,
Patrick Marsden
Continuity
Bunny Parsons
Director of photography
Jack Cardiff FRPS
Camera operators
Geoffrey Unsworth,
Christopher Challis
Focus pullers
Christopher Challis,
Eric Besche
Clapper loader
D. R. E. Allport
Motorbike shots
Michael Chorlton
Chief electrician
Bill Wall
Colour control
Natalie Kalmus
Associate colour control
Joan Bridge
**Special photographic
effects**
Douglas Woolsey, Henry
Harris, Technicolor Ltd

**Additional special
effects**
W. Percy Day, George
Blackwell, Stanley Grant
Back projection
Stanley Whitehead
Production designer
Alfred Junge
Assistant art director
Arthur Lawson
Draughtsmen
W. Hutchinson, Don Picton,
William Kellner
Editor
Reginald Mills
Liaison editor
John Seabourne
Assistant editor
Dave Powell
Music
Allan Gray
Music conductor
Walter Goehr
**Assistant music
conductor**
W. L. Williamson
Sound recording
C. C. Stevens
Sound camera operator
Harold Rowland
Boom operator
Dave Hildyard
Sound maintenance
Roy Day
Dubbing crew
Desmond Dew,
Alan Whatley
Costumes
Hein Heckroth
Make-up
George Blackler
Hair
Ida Mills
Table-tennis trainer
Alan Brook
**Operating theatre
technical adviser**
Capt. Bernard Kaplan RAMC
Stills
Eric Gray

104 mins
9371 feet

David Niven
Peter David Carter
Kim Hunter
June
Robert Coote
Bob Trubshaw
Kathleen Byron
An officer angel
Richard Attenborough
An English pilot
Bonar Colleano
Flying Fortress Captain
Joan Maude
Chief Recorder
Marius Goring
Conductor 71
Roger Livesey
Dr Frank Reeves
Robert Atkins
Vicar
Bob Roberts
Dr Gaertler
Edwin Max
Dr McEwen
Betty Potter
Mrs Tucker
Abraham Sofaer
The judge/the surgeon
Raymond Massey
Abraham Farlan
Tommy Duggan
American policeman
Roger Snowden
Irishman
Robert Arden
GI
Joan Verney
Girl
Wendy Thompson
Nurse
Wally Patch
ARP Warden

ALSO PUBLISHED

If you would like further information about future BFI Film Classics or about other books on film, media and popular culture from BFI Publishing, please write to:

**BFI Film Classics
BFI Publishing
21 Stephen Street
London W1P 2LN**